The Empowerment Model

of Clinical Supervision

A roadmap through the complexities of community mental health

Khara Croswaite Brindle

Christina Murphy

Acknowledgments

Thank you to the wonderful individuals who supported us through this journey to make this book possible! We couldn't have done it without the help of Lea Ayer, Jack Balnave, Sean Jacobsen, Kyra Logsdon, Laura Malmgren, Jessica Rock, Cassandra Williams, and the Griffith Centers for Children CHINS UP program staff.

Foreword

Welcome both counselors and supervisors to our book on empowerment within clinical supervision! While working in community mental health and serving clients of diverse backgrounds, we've identified a unique need to address the adventures and challenges of clinical mental health in community settings. This need comes from the awareness that community mental health agencies are large, fast-paced service organizations supporting new professionals and at-risk clients alike. For example, it takes specific skills to navigate community resources, agency protocols, and collaboration with community partners while maintaining a high volume of clients. Therefore, we wanted to highlight some of the dynamic needs of supporting professionals in these arenas through an engaging, supportive, empowering supervision model. We hope you find the material in this book rich in information regarding clinical supervision needs in community mental health. The more than 30 vignettes included are intended to explore some of the fascinating challenges of navigating confidentiality and crisis in community settings and are included to encourage critical thinking from a place of curiosity and learned experience. We also hope the content featured here inspires discussion and growth while fostering positive relationships between supervisor and supervisee. Lastly, we hope this book can support seasoned supervisors, aspiring supervisors, and new counselors alike. We see this book as a heartfelt effort to achieve best practice in professional collaboration within supervisory relationships in order to promote empowerment and growth within our shared communities.

Chapter Outline

Introduction to Clinical Supervision

Clinical supervision has always been a key component in helping professionals, but it has only recently gained more attention as a distinct field that is necessary to provide counselors in training with clinical and professional skills. More specifically, the knowledge and practical training that is acquired through supervision helps trainees become effective, competent, and ethical counselors. Master's and doctoral programs in counseling equip learners with information that is pertinent to clinical supervision, but it is only over the past 20 years that supervision has become an area of specialized training for postgraduates. Prior to the establishment of this specific field, most supervisory relationships were informal and lacked formal documentation procedures, the guidelines were minimal, and too much emphasis was placed on the number of supervision-related hours (Haynes, Gerald, & Moulton, (2002).

This field has dramatically changed over time, with licensed supervisors undergoing formal supervision training, which includes proper documentation practices. Furthermore, the Council for Accreditation of Counseling and Related Education Programs (CACREP, 2001), focuses on counseling, lifespan, and career development theories; ethical and legal standards; social and multicultural concepts; family and group counseling; assessment instruments; research and intervention evaluation; and consulting skills that afford supervisees with a sound understanding of how they can work with clients. Supervisory tasks also include guiding supervisees, protecting the welfare of clients, and serving as gatekeepers for this field. Therefore, clinical supervision integrates various aspects of professional development, thereby facilitating and enhancing the application of key counseling concepts. Accordingly, this chapter will provide a definition of clinical supervision, a discussion of the manner in which this field has evolved, a description of the purpose of supervision, and the aims for supervisees. Vignettes of clinical challenges that require supervision will be offered as well as a means of illustrating how specific issues may be competently and ethically addressed.

Clinical Supervision - Defined

Clinical supervision is defined as guided direction from a supervisor that promotes self-assessment, growth, and active involvement efforts that enhance counseling abilities and skills (Borders & Brown, 2005; Landany, Mori, & Mehr, 2013). It is also referred to as a unique triadic system as it involves the professional relationship between the supervisor, supervisee, and the clients being served (Bernard & Goodyear, 2009). The general aim of clinical supervision is to provide counselors in training with increasing competence in practicing the skills of their profession so that they will gradually require less direction from a supervisor. This is facilitated through the distinct balance between professional development opportunities that the supervisor creates and the hedge of protection for the clients that the supervisee serves (Haynes et al., 2002).

Supervisees, in particular, may have received limited feedback on their counseling skills during their academic career and they may still be in the process of trying to understand how to apply the theories, skills, and techniques they learned during their counseling program. This may be especially true for most post-master's students who recently graduated and are seeking supervision. As a result, counselors in training may vary widely in terms of their professional behavior, counseling skills, competence, and even career goals, which makes the specialized field known as clinical supervision especially important. Academic programs provide a wealth of information about counseling in theory, however, specific guidance from a well-experienced supervisor affords a better understanding of how to apply actual counseling practices as well as ways to address difficult situations that often arise in clinical sessions.

The supervisor plays an important role in observing which counseling skills supervisees are using as well as those which are not being applied, a supervisee's level of comfort with various clients and clinical problems, and session pacing. Additional aspects of supervision entail displaying openness to supervisory feedback and learning how to address apprehensions related to practice.

Specific objectives for supervisees include:

- Acquiring competence and self-confidence through increased counseling practice

- Expanding skills despite the risk of making mistakes through discussions and guidance from a supervisor
- Developing the capacity to evaluate both the professional and personal role as a counselor
- Gradually enhancing the practice of self-evaluation

Interestingly, licensed supervisors often report that counselors in training possess a plethora of educated intuition and insights, but usually do not trust their intuition, feelings, or knowledge to properly guide them in practice (Haynes et al., 2002). Therefore, clinical supervision provides support which encourages supervisees to apply their previously acquired knowledge and skills in a manner that promotes professional growth and development. This form of supervision also becomes a platform for monitoring performance that subsequently empowers supervisees to face new insights about themselves, establish new perspectives and behaviors, learn how to self-supervise, and to gradually carry out competent counseling practices as an independent helping professional (Haynes et al., 2002).

Currently, postgraduate students, especially post-master's students, may be hesitant in terms of participating in supervision. A limited understanding of how essential this form of directed guidance is may be contributing to this trend. Another potential factor could be that previous negative experiences from the supervisory relationship are hindering a clinician's ability to engage freely during subsequent interactions. Accordingly, one focal point of this book is to provide insight regarding the structure and importance of seeking clinical supervision upon degree completion. It is not enough to learn the theory and ethics of counseling, trainees must gain experience about situations that will appropriately translate into independent practice in the future. Clinical supervision facilitates this essential process.

Overview of Clinical Supervision

Education requirements

The education requirement for clinical supervision is a master's degree or higher in a mental health field. The degree must be obtained from a post-secondary educational institution, a program accredited by an accrediting agency (e.g., CACREP, APA), or a program that received state approval from an agency that is recognized by the U.S. Secretary of Education. Degrees that were earned outside of the U.S. will have to be evaluated by an international transcript assessment service and the results must be submitted to the Center for Credentialing and Education (CCE). Each mental health discipline has specific clinical supervision requirements that must be met prior to licensure. Therefore, it is important to carefully review licensure requirements.

Licensure Requirements

The length of the clinical supervision period for supervisees is dependent upon educational level and state licensing board requirements. It is important to keep in mind that licensure requirements vary per licensure type and state. The chosen supervisor should be a licensed counselor, marriage and family therapist, psychologist, social worker, or additional helping professional that a board deems eligible to provide supervision. It is standard practice for supervisors to pursue the highest level of licensing or credentialing deemed appropriate by each state in which the individual holds the role of supervisor.

Supervision Modalities

The needs of community programs can be met by offering specific modalities such as reflective supervision, person-centered supervision, and psychodynamic supervision. *Reflective supervision* involves a supervisory relationship that focuses on the influence that one relationship may have upon another and the potential impact of parallel processes (Hornby Zeller Associates, 2014). It also places emphasis on empowering a supervisee to identify solutions or make decisions by actively using strategies that are learned during the supervision process such as listening, contemplating, and waiting.

The key elements of reflective supervision include regularly scheduled, face-to-face meetings between the supervisee and supervisor, which aim at encouraging reflection on counseling behavior and the application of improved skills during subsequent sessions. However, the meetings are also a platform where concerns can be discussed and corrective plans can be developed, if necessary. An essential component of reflective supervision is the frequency of the supervisory meetings, which should be at least monthly, but can also be weekly or every two weeks.

This structured modality helps promote an open line of communication that is intended to establish strong supervisory rapport, increase retention, and provide opportunities for supervisees to experience enhanced levels of self-reflection that boost competence and confidence in their role as a helping professional (Stinchfield, Hill, & Kleist, 2007). In addition, it aims at creating a safe, calm, and supportive environment where supervisees can do their best thinking and express their honest opinions. Accordingly, this type of supervision promotes a trainee's reflective capacity, which specifically refers to the ability to assess personal feelings, actions, reactions, and thoughts that are evoked during sessions. Several examples of scenarios pertaining to confidentiality-related situations that counselors may struggle to discuss with their supervisors are included below.

Additionally, reflection entails taking a temporary break from intense counseling to contemplate what the training experiences really mean as well as what the sessions reveal about the clients. By doing so, interventions that best meet a client's goals for growth and self-sufficiency can be identified and supervisees can also manage counseling-related stress in a constructive manner by working through complex feelings. Subsequently, supervisees gradually become well-versed in the reflective process and mastery in their particular field will also improve. Indeed, supervisees tend to report that this form of supervision creates a supportive work environment in which supervisors and even fellow supervisees are readily available to help address concerns (Hornby Zeller Associates, 2014). Therefore, reflective supervision entails positive, productive meetings which encourage innovative thinking and allows supervisees to work through difficult situations without the fear of being judged. They also receive guidance and feedback that promotes reflection and professional advancement. Similar to reflective supervision, ***person-centered supervision*** supports the perspective that individuals have the capacity to direct their own lives and resolve their own problems (Haynes, Corey, & Moulton, 2003).

In particular, person-centered supervision focuses on establishing a working relationship in which a supervisee is encouraged to use his or her resources (e.g., previous knowledge and experience) to promote professional and personal growth. It entails Socratic questioning (Overholser, 2018), which is defined as a disciplined practice that enables trainees to examine the logic of their ideas in order to determine their validity. It is also based on building a warm, trusting, safe, and empathetic supervisory relationship. However, in contrast to reflective supervision which entails scaffolded instruction that can lessen and be removed when mastery is achieved (Feldman, 2016), the person-centered approach supports ongoing collaboration that encourages supervisees to think critically and conceptualize their cases. That is, the supervisee directs meetings and presents topics that need to be discussed, while the supervisor provides opinions that enhance a supervisee's ability to assess how optimized services can be offered to their clients. In doing so, the supervisor plays a larger role in facilitating development than being a gatekeeper or evaluator. Examples of questions and statements a supervisor may use to facilitate person-centered supervision include:

- What are your objectives for today's supervision meeting?
- Tell me about your experience while counseling that client.
- What aspects of the session with the client were important to discuss today?
- Describe the type of relationship you would like to establish with the client?
- What approach do you think would best help the client?
- Do you feel like you understand the client well?
- How can I encourage you to trust your own judgement more often?
- Tell me about a challenging session and what that looked like for you?

Although this process is intended to guide supervisees to find the answers to their own questions, it is sometimes argued that person-centered supervision does not meet the legal and ethical standards of helping professions (Weiner & Craighead, 2009). In particular, emphasis is generally placed on supervisees learning how to resolve their own counseling needs and this may prevent the welfare of the client from being a priority in some cases. Subsequently, a client may not receive intervention that is optimal for his or her situation. Despite this potential limitation, the benefits of person-centered supervision include the ability to promote self-discovery, build confidence, enhance problem-solving skills, and reduce anxiety for struggling supervisees (Bernard & Goodyear, 2009; Wong, Wong, & Ishiyama, 2012). Furthermore, when this form of supervision is implemented effectively, a supervisee should be able to efficiently apply person-centered therapy, which places the primary focus on the client.

Indeed, this approach involves displaying empathy toward clients when they are discussing their emotions. In a therapeutic setting, a helping professional actively listens while a client communicates, and then conveys understanding that encourages the individual to confide more details which may reveal underlying issues that are contributing to the client's problems. This in turn becomes an interaction in which the helping professional (e.g., supervisee) is a sensitive, respectful, and warm companion that provides support during the difficult exploration of another person's emotional world (Bernard & Goodyear, 2009). In support of the client, the supervisee's response should remain neutral and unaffected, as this type of counseling practice was learned during person-centered supervision. This particular form of training gives supervisees a significant level of autonomy, but it is structured in a manner that facilitates openness which should indicate when a supervisee needs to make adjustments to his or her counseling practices. In addition, the regularly scheduled supervisory meetings should also reveal whether a problem is developing during sessions in order for a supervisor to make immediate recommendations in the form of Socratic questioning that would lead to a resolution and protect the client's welfare. Therefore, both reflective supervision and person-centered supervision share important similarities that promote efficient counseling practice and services.

Psychodynamic supervision is a third modality of supervision that draws on clinical research which is inherent to theoretical orientations of the mental health field (e.g., defense mechanisms, affective reactions, transference, countertransference, etc.). Interestingly, psychodynamic supervision is further classified into three categories: client-centered, supervisee-centered, and supervisory-matrix centered.

The *client-centered* category directs the supervision session toward a client's verbal and behavioral presentation. There are several techniques that facilitate client-centered psychodynamic therapy. These include:

- Ensuring that strong therapeutic rapport is established
- Paying close attention to a client's expression of emotions
- Identifying repetitive patterns in a client's life or relationships
- Placing emphasis on past experiences
- Exploring a client's dreams, goals, and wishes
- Focusing on a client's interpersonal experiences
- Exploring a client's resistance or attempts to avoid certain topics

Additional characteristics that are specific to psychodynamic supervision involve setting a time limitation on the intervention (e.g., 12-40 sessions) and targeting one interpersonal problem to address during the first few sessions (Bomba, 2011). An example of how a psychodynamic supervisee may address a sensitive situation is as follows: "I noticed during the last two sessions that when I ask you about your feelings, you tend to become silent and look way. Did you realize that this was happening? Is this an especially painful topic for you to discuss? Is there a way I can help make this issue more bearable for you to talk about?" In this case, confrontation and interpretation are applied in an empathetic manner that aims at helping the client gain awareness and become more open to resolving personal issues. The supervisor also plays a didactic role in this process in order to help supervisees understand and properly address their clients' needs. That is, the supervisor is a consultant who is not directly involved in the counseling sessions, but offers skills and knowledge that assist the supervisee. In regard to the training environment, as the primary focus is on the client and not the supervisory relationship, very little conflict develops between the supervisee and supervisor as long as they agree regarding the interpretation of the theoretical orientation. In addition, the lack of stress or conflict during the supervision meetings typically reduces a supervisee's anxiety and fosters enhanced learning (Bomba, 2011).

In contrast to client-centered practices, *supervisee-centered* psychodynamic supervision focuses on the process and content of a supervisee's experience as a helping professional (Falender & Shafranske, 2008). It specifically places emphasis on common issues supervisees face such as anxiety, resistance, and learning problems. The supervisor is still the authoritative, uninvolved consultant, but this training approach is less didactic and more experiential as the attention is slightly shifted away from the client to the psychology of the supervisees' experiences (Falender & Shafranska, 2004; Frawley-O'Dea & Sarnat, 2001). Accordingly, this form of training supports professional growth by promoting a sound understanding of personal and psychological processes that influence a supervisee's counseling practices. However, some supervisees feel as though this approach results in more scrutiny and subsequent stress.

The *supervisory-matrix centered* method of supervision attends to the client's case, the supervisee's experiences, and the supervisory relationship. More specifically, this is a relational approach in which the supervisor actively participates in, reflects upon, and evaluates the effective use of enactments (Ladany et al., 2013). The supervisor also interprets relational situations that develop during supervisory or counseling sessions, and this includes the potential occurrence of parallel processes. Therefore, this method offers a significant level of flexibility in terms of the way services may be provided to clients.

In summary, the psychodynamic modality ensures that supervision incorporates the theoretical orientation of the field with the application of generic therapeutic skills and it also aims at furthering the development and maintenance of skills that are specifically associated with psychodynamic therapy (Bomba, 2011). Newer models of supervision also promote the advancement of the mental health field and afford supervisors, supervisees, and clients with optimal learning platforms and interventions.

Administrative versus Clinical Supervision

Professional development includes both counselor competencies and ethical guidelines that require exploration and resulting documentation. The two general categories of supervision are known as administrative and clinical.

Administrative supervision places emphasis on a supervisee's professional role and responsibilities in his or her chosen field (e.g., Association of Marriage and Family Therapy, social work, etc.) and additional matters such as personal issues (e.g., approved leave), documentation, productivity, staff meetings, and timekeeping (Bradley & Kottler, 2001). In addition, administrative supervision focuses on the different types of clinical programs within the organization of which the supervisor and supervisee are affiliated (Kreider, 2014). In regard to administration, the supervisor is also viewed as the supervisee's manager (Tromski-Klingshirn, 2007). Additional aspects that fall under administrative supervision include (Haynes et al., 2002):

- Problem solving
- Communications

- Time management
- Performance appraisal
- Oversight of accreditation
- Billing and budgetary matters
- Maintenance of ethical and legal standards
- Overseeing staff cultural competence issues
- Compliance with state and federal regulations
- Quality control and improvement, problem solving
- Human resources management (e.g., hiring, disciplining, firing)

However, one of the most critical components for an administrative supervisor is documentation. This task is crucial to risk-management and it is the key link between work performance and rendering services effectively. The following records of supervision are required (See Appendices):

- A signed supervisor-supervisee contract
- A summary of the supervisee's training, experience, and learning objectives
- A current Individual Development Plan (IDP)
- A summary of the supervisee's performance evaluations

- Notation of missed or cancelled supervision sessions
- Progressive disciplinary actions, if necessary
- Clinical recommendations the supervisor made for the supervisee
- Significant problems that occurred during supervision and the resolutions
- Session notes, including discussions of sensitive cases and decisions that were made

Clinical supervision in comparison, is overseeing a supervisee's work skills when services are being provided to clients. In the broader sense, clinical supervision involves the continuous observation and evaluation of a supervisee's counseling practices. However, it also entails an assessment of counseling skill efficacy, the ability to address ethical issues, case conceptualization, and the client-counselor relationship (ACES, 2011; Tromski-Klingshirn, 2007). Ultimately clinical supervision affords supervisees with the following (SAMHSA, 2009):

- Enhanced professionalization
- Improved intervention effectiveness
- Increased workforce satisfaction
- Improved counselor efficiency

- Enhanced quality of client services
- Increased counselor and client retention rates
- Assurance that the services provided adhere to ethical standards and legal mandates

Furthermore, the clinical aspect of supervision has been referred to as a central organizing body that integrates a program's intervention philosophy, goals, and mission with clinical theories and evidence based-practices. Its structure also encourages supervision to be adjusted to the experience, skills, knowledge base, and assignment of each supervisee. Most importantly, the supervisor needs to demonstrate sound legal and ethical practices within the supervisory relationship as this is how proper counseling strategies are translated from a concept to a regular set of behaviors. That is, supervisees can observe their supervisors in order to develop a process of ethical problem solving and decision-making skills that can be used when new situations are encountered. In other words, even supervisees who feel as if they already have years of experience can benefit from quality clinical supervision.

Although these are two distinct categories of supervision, they share several similarities. For instance, the role of both the administrative and clinical supervisor is to provide evaluation and feedback, but the outcomes of the evaluations may vary greatly. In particular, administrative assessments may influence employment or compensation decisions, while clinical assessments support professional development and self-evaluation. Furthermore, tasks such as reviewing clients' cases, discussing areas of strength and weakness, and addressing ethical issues are also carried out in a similar manner during the administrative and clinical sessions (Kreider, 2014). There is indeed an overlap in responsibilities in both administrative and clinical supervision, but the purpose of these activities is quite different. In particular, the purpose of evaluation and feedback from an administrative supervisor is to ensure that supervisees are adhering to program policies, following ethical guidelines, and are functioning as efficient employees. The clinical supervisor's primary aim, however, is to promote supervisee growth and to ensure the protection of each client's welfare.

Some supervisors may decide to take on a dual role in which they must carefully assess a supervisee's practical performance and policy adherence, while simultaneously establishing rapport that facilitates effective supervision (Lampropoulos, 2002). In general, dual-role supervision affords trainees with increased contact with their supervisor in opposition to having to divide time between an administrative supervisor and a clinical supervisor. Dual-role supervisors may be in place due to limited resources within agencies in response to financial limitations and a desire for efficiency. According to one study, dual-role supervisors demonstrate more thorough administrative oversight of clinical cases (Tromski-Klingshirn & Davis, 2007). Furthermore, most supervisees do not view dual-role supervision as problematic and in some cases, it may be required (Tromski-Klingshirn & Davis, 2007).

In order for effective supervision to take place, supervisees need to disclose their counseling experiences (Walsh et al., 2003), especially when difficulties arise such as discussions involving suicidal ideations or anticipated acts of physical harm. Indeed, supervisee disclosure is an essential aspect of supervision, professional growth, and self-evaluation, but it relies on trainees discussing cases they may be struggling with during supervision where live observation or immediate supervisor support may not be available. However, research indicates that supervisees frequently withhold information from their supervisors for a number of reasons that include a fear of impression management or professional repercussions (Mehr, Ladany, & Caskie, 2010).

When a clinical supervisor takes on the administrative role, a supervisee may be hesitant to disclose information about sensitive issues that were discussed during counseling sessions. Fear and reluctance subsequently impedes upon a supervisee's ability to make progress and also can put clients' welfare at risk if critical information (e.g., suicidal thoughts) is not disclosed to a supervisor. This hesitation to disclose also alludes to an even bigger issue, which is the general lack of engagement in appropriate supervision among post-graduates, especially post-master's graduates in response to concerns of competency. These reservations are understandable when exploring supervisee concerns regarding negative evaluations or apprehensions pertaining to self-sufficiency as a competent professional.

Implications for Licensed Supervisors

As mentioned previously, post-master's mental health professionals have varying degrees of experience and exposure to supervisory relationships. One of the key aspects of clinical supervision involves the supervisor's role in helping a supervisee develop the ability to self-supervise and eventually take over the supervisory task (Bernard & Goodyear, 2009). This means that in addition to guiding supervisees, protecting the welfare of clients, and serving as gatekeepers for this field, the main goal of the supervisor is to assist supervisees with developing the skills and awareness they need for self-evaluation. In order to facilitate this process, supervisees are given opportunities to apply their decision-making and problem-solving skills as well as practice self-supervision and self-evaluation. That is, by providing supervision during a counseling session as well as feedback and constructive criticism when necessary, a supervisor helps trainees learn how to trust their own clinical judgement. In doing so, the trainees become empowered, competent practitioners who are able to monitor their own performance, identify personal issues that may affect counseling practices, and recognize the limits of their competence as well as when to seek additional supervision.

The aforementioned content reflects a supervisor's primary role, but if a conflict arises between training a supervisee and protecting a client's welfare, ethic codes dictate that the welfare of the client becomes a priority. For instance, if a supervisee reports that a client discussed thoughts of suicide during a session, then the supervision rapidly shifts from training the supervisee to placing immediate attention on the client around the concern of suicidal ideation. However, the focus of supervision may shift temporarily until the crisis has been resolved. The supervisor may subsequently resume the training by teaching about suicide assessment and intervention. By carefully addressing these types of sensitive situations, supervision can engage a supervisee in exploration of critical incidents, allowing increased awareness and confidence in intervention.

Another complexity of roles that may arise is known as a parallel process, where a supervisee may, for example, inadvertently supervise clients or the structure of a session while being supervised (Borders & Brown, 2005).

In such cases, professional progress often becomes limited or dormant as the supervisee is mimicking the supervisor as opposed to further developing counseling and self-evaluation skills. However, resolving the transference impasse in the supervisory relationship typically resolves the parallelism that was occurring during the counseling sessions. This may be achieved by redirecting the sessions through the use of a specific agenda and a description of how the session will be conducted. Redirection helps supervisees return their focus to serving the clients instead of unintentionally supervising their clients.

Supervisors may also experience this type of parallelism. For instance, feelings of frustration that a supervisor may have with one supervisee could affect the supervisory relationship with a different supervisee. Thusly, negative dynamics can be transferred from one supervisory session to another and this could impede upon a supervisee's ability to make progress. Once again, it becomes the supervisor's responsibility to recognize and offer solutions to this type of situation.

In regard to cases such as these, proficient supervisors will take the necessary steps to ensure that ethical and professional issues do not interfere with their ability to supervise, and as the training continues, the supervisee will consistently acquire competence and self-confidence. Accordingly, supervisors who have a clear understanding of a trainee's goals and establish specific objectives for the supervision period help trainees develop the ability to evaluate their own personal role as a counselor. Evaluation can take place through live observation, video review, or audio transcription of a trainee's work. Overall, supervisors who have specific training strategies and can communicate the corresponding objectives effectively can afford their trainees with beneficial supervision that facilitates professional development.

Challenges to Consider in Supervision

There are several factors that may impede the supervision process and these include: personal issues that haven't been addressed, resistance to feedback, and a lack of motivation (Inman et al., 2014). However, another issue that may develop is ***transference***, which occurs when a supervisee's positive or negative feelings of interpersonal interactions (e.g., parent-child, friendships, or romantic relationships) are brought into the supervisory relationship. Countertransference is the term that is used to describe the same situation in reference to supervisors. In regard to the supervisee, the occurrence of transference typically describes the supervisee displacing and projecting teaching behavior in clinical settings. Accordingly, when a supervisor is alert and aware of what is happening, transference can inform the training professional of problematic scenarios a trainee may unconsciously enact with clients. A supervisee may also display the same behavior during supervisory meetings (Fink, 2007). The following is an example of transference in supervision:

A supervisee receives training from a supervisor whose empathic personality and non-judgmental tone evokes positive feelings from childhood and, over time, results in the supervisor being viewed as a mother figure (Fink, 2007). The supervisee subsequently displays an enhanced capacity and willingness to learn, but not for the sole purpose of gaining clinical experience. That is, the feelings of maternal attachment that have developed increase the supervisee's motivation to engage in training out of a desire to please or gain approval from the supervisor.

A supervisor's decision to address this issue and the strategy that is used depends exclusively upon the situation (Fink. 2007). For instance, if the supervisor recognizes this form of transference or intrapsychic conflict, but also notices that the supervisee's counseling performance improves, it may be determined that this form of attachment has enhanced the supervisee's ability to establish professional rapport with clients and the supervisor may decide not to openly address the transference with the supervisee. However, if the supervisee begins to engage in inappropriate or excessive self-disclosure (e.g., talking about a romantic date and seeking advice) during supervisory meetings, the transference would need to be addressed and resolved as the same pattern of behavior may be displayed in clinical settings. More specifically, the supervisee may divulge personal information with clients or expect clients to disclose such information as well, thereby violating ethical principles regarding protecting the welfare of clients. Indeed, this type of situation poses questions regarding the trainee's ethical considerations of the client's welfare and displays a lack of focus on the client's clinical needs. A trainee's personal matters are irrelevant to the client's case and are therefore inappropriate to discuss during counseling sessions. Furthermore, this type of transference indicates that the trainee's clinical work is no longer in alignment with the therapeutic goals that were established for the client's case.

In general, transference enactments can influence clinical supervision regardless of whether a supervisee or supervisor consciously acknowledges their occurrence. Supervisors who recognize such enactments are typically better able to understand the underlying issues that may interfere with a supervisee's ability to relate to their clients. Additionally, the supervisory process improves markedly when a supervisor actively studies manifestations of transference and responds to them correctively. Properly facilitated corrective interventions also promote self-reflective and relational capacities of supervisees (Schamess, 2006).

Supervisee anxiety is another common factor that may affect a trainee's counseling practices. In particular, most supervisees will experience some level of anxiety about their clinical supervision training and their ability to work well with clients (Haynes et al., 2003). The majority of supervisees typically excelled during their academic programs, but beginning to apply that knowledge in practical settings can quickly cause anxiety levels to rise. Similarly, the idea of being evaluated by a supervisor may also lead to unexpected distress. However, supervisors who are open, honest, and non-judgmental can help supervisees effectively manage their anxiety (Haynes et al., 2003). In addition, supervisors who share their experiences about challenges they faced during training can help reduce supervisees' apprehensions. These types of revelations help trainees realize that they are not alone in their struggles and also shows them that making mistakes is common and unavoidable. Additionally, it should allow them to feel more comfortable when discussing their mistakes during supervisory meetings. Addressing supervisees as colleagues during such times can also encourage them to trust their abilities to learn and practice competently as helping professionals.

Limited Supervision in our Communities

There are a number of reasons why post-graduates are often reluctant to seek out clinical supervision. Factors that most often contribute to this issue include a fear of having to disclose personal matters that may affect client services or sensitive information a client discussed during a session, apprehensions regarding evaluation and feedback, and repercussions that could be potentially experienced (Mehr et al., 2010). There are also post-graduates who may have already gained counseling experience and as a result, may feel as if they do not need supervision. This is oftentimes the case for post-doctoral graduates who received experience during or directly after completing their program, although some post-master's graduates also begin obtaining experience shortly after ending their program. Nonetheless, for supervisees who begin training, but display defensiveness, fearfulness, or anxiousness, self-disclosure by the supervisor regarding counseling struggles and successes, personal issues, non-counseling-related professional experiences, etc., can help supervisees overcome their resistance to supervision (Kreider, 2014).

Limited access to professionals who can provide efficient supervision is another problem that is contributing to the lack of clinical supervision in our communities. For instance, research indicates that school counselors who work in rural areas are in many cases the only mental health provider in their community and they do not always have access to their supervision needs (Bardhoshi & Duncan, 2009). Furthermore, mental health needs in rural areas are described as being greater than the amount of resources that are available and counselors suggest that more mental health training would close this gap (Bain et al., 2011). Other helping professionals in different mental health fields may also struggle to find well-trained, licensed supervisors who can offer the level of supervision that is needed for professional growth. Additionally, in community mental health centers where the choice of supervisors may be limited, the clinical counseling supervisor that is chosen for training purposes may have a similar level of credentials and skills as the supervisee. This limit in accessibility to licensed professionals makes it more difficult to receive supervision from a licensed supervisor with years of expertise and experience. In response to these limitations, it is proposed that the use of technology (e.g., video conferencing) may help facilitate supervision for professionals in remote areas, as one example (Duncan, Brown-Rice, & Bardhoshi, 2014).

Additional suggestions that allow greater access to supervision include summer courses, weekend workshops, or cooperative in-service programs as well as collaborative efforts between university training programs and professional state organizations. It has even been argued that supervision training should be incorporated as a requirement for master's level training programs (Duncan et al., 2014). Therefore, the creation of efficient and effective statewide clinical supervision plans may promote access and willingness to participate in such programs. More importantly, supervision program needs should be tailored to the community's needs.

Empowerment in Clinical Supervision

An empowerment modality of supervision is based on the premise that mental health organizations encourage autonomous decision making among the helping professionals who are closest to the issues and problems their clients face. It also promotes addressing challenges in unique ways that will ultimately help professionals grow and succeed. An additional aim of this model of supervision is to assist supervisees as they progress through various developmental stages and tasks that allow them to establish a counselor or therapist identity of their own, thereby replacing the external supervisor with an internal supervisor (Granello, Beamish, & Davis, 1997). That is, empowerment-focused supervision creates a setting in which supervisees can acquire the experience they need to become independent professionals through teaching, evaluation, consultation, advising, mentoring, coaching, and counseling (Bernard & Goodyear, 2009).

What is the Empowerment Model of Clinical Supervision?

The Empowerment Model of Clinical Supervision was established after numerous hours of clinical counseling were provided to interns and post master's counselors alike, as this led to the discovery that the more supervisees are empowered, the easier it is for them to a develop a strong supervisory relationship that is built on trust. It was also observed that this form of empowerment leads to more competent counselors by the end of the supervision experience.

This Model also places emphasis on the different roles that supervisors naturally move through with new counselors. For instance, a supervisor may be a teacher at one point and a consultant at another, with the main goal of supervision involving the advancement of counselor's skills with the goal that he or she reaches the level of a colleague within their professional development (Borders & Brown, 2005). It is also important to note that in conjunction with exemplifying each of the supervisory roles (e.g., teacher, researcher, consultant, etc.), the supervisor focuses on empowering counselors at each developmental step and customizes the supervision to each individual counselor's level of experience and/or expertise. Accordingly, this model focuses on the manner in which a clinical supervisor can recognize the different development levels of supervisees and promote their continuous progression. This is the key component to equipping counselors with individualized supervision that empowers them to meet their full potential. The Empowerment Model's emphasis of individualized, developmental supervision also makes it distinct from the more conventional clinical supervision approaches.

What Makes This Model Different?

The basis of clinical supervision is to ensure that new counselors acquire the skills they need to provide counseling in a competent, professional, and ethical manner that is in accordance with their organization's mission. Subsequently, once graduates seek clinical supervision, they are typically viewed as novice counselors who are starting out at the same level and should therefore receive a conventional or standardized form of clinical supervision. It has been observed, however, that supervisees tend to vary widely in terms of their developmental level, actual experience, and expertise.

Therefore, this model encourages supervisors to recognize supervisees who may have advanced skills as well as those who may require more foundational elements in their professional development in order to start clinical supervision at the identified and appropriate developmental level.

Accordingly, the role a supervisor initially takes on can be influenced by a supervisee's level of skills at the start of clinical supervision, and the movement between each role remains fluid. This means that a supervisor may be a teacher early on in supervision for one supervisee, but may begin at a consultant level for a different supervisee due to recognition that they have a higher developmental level and understanding of counseling. Furthermore, this model ensures that a supervisor does not remain within a certain role for an extended period just because a supervisee is a novice counselor. Instead it encourages supervisors to freely move through the different roles based on the counseling needs that have been identified for the supervisee. For instance, a licensed supervisee may have obtained the required number of training hours and passed the licensing exam but may not have ample experience with providing counseling to clients with distinct issues (e.g., marital problems, substance abuse disorder). In this case, although the counselor is licensed, he or she would still need to be taught new counseling skills, thereby making it necessary for the supervisor to take on a teaching role. Therefore, this model is unique in that involves assessing each supervisee's developmental and counseling level before providing supervision as well as recognizing when to move into different roles to accommodate various counseling situations once supervision begins.

In order to apply The Empowerment Model, a supervisee's clinical supervision needs must first be identified through the administration of the Supervision Evaluation, a tool that has been adapted from Griffith Centers for Children, a non-profit organization offering therapeutic services to diverse communities in Colorado (please see Appendix A). The evaluation is divided into five sections: general supervision, administrative counseling, clinical counseling, the conceptualization process, and professional communication.

Evaluation items that pertain to *general supervision* include an assessment of whether the supervisee:

- Demonstrates a personal commitment to developing professional competencies.
- Invests time and energy in becoming a proficient therapist.
- Accepts and uses feedback to enhance self-development and counseling skills.
- Engages in open, comfortable, and clear communication with their supervisor.

Items related to ***administrative counseling*** include making sure the supervisee:

- Researches the referral prior to intake.
- Keeps appointments on time, has minimal cancelations/reschedules.
- Schedules intake promptly.
- Explains the nature and objective of services when necessary.

The following items reflect those that are used for the assessment of ***clinical counseling*** skills:

- Facilitates clients' expressions of concerns and feelings.
- Focuses on the content of the client's problems.

- Recognizes clients' maladaptive behaviors and responds appropriately.
- Is aware of own feelings during sessions.

Several of the items that reflect the *conceptualization process* are as follows:

- Focuses on specific behaviors and their consequences.
- Recognizes and pursues descriptions and meaning of inconsistent information.
- Uses relevant case data in planning both immediate and long-range goals.
- Uses relevant case data in considering various strategies and their implications.
- Applies theoretical orientation to identify appropriate diagnosis and treatment goals.

Finally, *professional communication* is assessed by observing whether the supervisee:

- Communicates with the professional team to move a case forward.
- Emails monthly reports/updates on time to the professional team.

- Notifies the professional team of referral assignment in a timely manner.
- Emails the professional team as needed to communicate concerns.
- Represents the agency mission and vision.
- Consistently demonstrates timely completion.

The Empowerment Model's Supervision Evaluation is comprised of 39 items, each of which is rated on a scale of 1 to 5 with (1 = Requires Intervention; 5 = Exceeds Expectations). Each supervisee is encouraged to complete the Supervision Evaluation for themselves. The supervisor will also complete a copy. The evaluations are reviewed in a supervision meeting and periodically thereafter to identify goals and goal progression within the supervisory relationship. The final score for each section reflects a supervisee's current level of skills and indicates where clinical supervision should begin in regard to a supervisor's role (e.g. teacher, consultant, researcher, etc.).

Figure 1.1 The Empowerment Model of Clinical
Supervision

As previously mentioned, the roles a supervisor
demonstrates are fluid to meet a supervisee's needs. An
especially important quality an empowerment-oriented
leader (supervisor) should possess is a willingness to
accept the diversity of their trainees, which includes
differences in motivation levels, counseling perspectives

and approaches, cultural views, etc. For instance, research has shown that supervisors who promote peer consultation and information exchange (e.g., through group sessions) afford trainees with increased personal empowerment and autonomy (Shera & Page, 1995).

If the results of the supervision assessment indicate that a supervisee needs to be taught specific skills, then the supervisor acts as the *teacher* by demonstrating how clinical skills can be effectively developed as well as utilizing training strategies that are consistent with the objectives and goals of clinical supervision. As a *researcher*, the supervisor employs analytical skills to assess a supervisee's previously acquired skills, progress throughout supervision, strengths that can be built upon, and weaknesses that can be addressed. A supervisor may even conduct research in order to observe and report about specific aspects of the clinical supervision of graduate students. This type of study may involve research components such as preparation for clinical supervision; continuing education with concurrent supervisees; institutional support for clinical supervisors; or training strategies that facilitate supervisees' clinical performance. The results could subsequently be used to advance the knowledge base of clinical supervision as well as for educational purposes for supervisors and supervisees.

A supervisor may also act as the **consultant**. At this point the supervisor has developed a strong level of trust with the supervisee and subsequently provides professional consultation when the supervisee presents a problem that occurred during a counseling session. Finally, when a supervisee reaches a proficient level of self-supervision, the supervisor becomes a **colleague** who can still provide support and guidance as needed. Regardless of the role demonstrated at the time of supervision, each of these roles revolves around the **individual self** and the **clinician self**. That is, it is important to ensure that factors associated with the individual self, such as personal issues, family or social problems, etc., do not impede upon aspects of the clinical self, such as professionalism, ethical competence, and integrity when a supervisor engages and interacts with a supervisee.

Furthermore, The Empowerment Model of Clinical Supervision posits that supervisors create optimal growing conditions by providing resources, learning and self-scaffolding opportunities, and support that motivate supervisees to play an active role in their own development, thusly allowing them to reach their potential (Ladany et al., 2013).

One particular model of reaching full potential is *the scaffolding model* (Zimmerman & Schunk, 2003). In particular, the concept of scaffolding is an interactive process in which supervisors encourage supervisees to apply prior knowledge and skills to promote new learning (Zimmerman & Schunk, 2003). As a supervisee demonstrates mastery of a specific stage, a supervisor can gradually adjust the scaffolded instruction to incorporate the skills and knowledge that facilitate learning at the next advanced stage while simultaneously encouraging the supervisee to apply the mastered knowledge and rely less on the supervision experience. During this process, the supervisee is progressively introduced to novel information and counseling strategies, but this supervisory interaction also helps trainees further develop their advanced critical thinking skills. Scaffolding is not a linear process as a supervisee may simultaneously be in different stages of the clinical training. Therefore, it is important to continuously assess a supervisee's developmental level. Scaffolding is eventually discontinued when a supervisee feels confident with his or her training and has mastered the required skills.

This type of structure supports autonomy as the supervisor is not to be viewed as an expert under The Empowerment Model, but is viewed instead as the authority who guides supervisees. The supervisor may teach specific clinical approaches, consult a supervisee regarding how to address culturally diverse clients, keep record during supervisory meetings, and offer a trainee evaluative feedback regarding his or her clinical progress.

The role of a supervisor changes depending on the situation, and competent supervisors have a clear understanding of when their role as well as the goals they wish to accomplish with their supervisees need, to be adjusted. Therefore, it is important to assess each situation to determine what form of supervision should be provided and what role should be demonstrated. Interestingly, in addition to the roles that have been described in literature in the past, 'empowerer' has been added as it is essential that a supervisor be able to help trainees learn how to handle challenges and ask for assistance through consultation when a problem arises (Haynes et al., 2003).

In doing so, a supervisee becomes empowered to apply self-supervision. However, this process is best initiated by a supervisor who acts as a guide and exercises leadership, which includes drawing on past experiences in order to demonstrate how clinical skills can be effectively developed.

In particular, *leadership* is defined as having the ability to influence the behavior of an individual or a group of people, and empowerment-oriented leaders (e.g., supervisors) are in an optimal position to inspire trainees of various professional backgrounds. Leaders also play an important role in establishing the vision of the organization as well as creating an organizational culture in which trainees become client-oriented and committed to values that support task-sharing. Additionally, they display the ability to motivate trainees by modeling appropriate behaviors and ethical values (Shera & Page, 1995). The leadership role also entails being responsible for sustaining supervisee morale and helping them with counseling-related discontents or discouragements. Furthermore, a strong leader provides supervisees with a sense of belonging to the organization, professional worth, and security with their performance.

In addition, research indicates that supervisees who have greater self-awareness, reflectivity, or cognitive complexity more readily utilize supervision efficiently and are better able to develop clinical skills specific to their profession (Inman et al., 2014). It was also reported that unresolved personal problems, limited motivation, and an unwillingness to accept feedback are characteristics that may impede a supervisee's development. Furthermore, supervisee empowerment research shows that more effective supervisees are proactive during supervision (e.g., observing other professionals), are more organized, and better prepared (e.g., discussing objectives for supervisory meetings) (Green et al., 2014). Indeed, those who are active participants in supervision bring helpful behaviors to the process such as orienting supervisors to their developmental needs, fostering learning alliances, and preparing themselves to aspire to ethical practices when challenging emotions are experienced. Several additional sources even suggest that it is important to empower supervisees to contribute in such ways. For instance, the American Psychological Association (APA) endorses the application of supervisee self-assessment for the purpose of strengthening supervisee's competence and reflective practice (APA, 2015).

The Empowerment Model in Action

Researchers also explain that empowerment in supervision elicits improved thinking, the processing of feedback, and self-care among supervisees (Falender & Shafranske, 2012). However, it is further suggested that this training approach is dynamically multifaceted and is the responsibility of both the supervisor and the supervisee. The shared responsibility encourages supervisees to deal with issues and resolve problems successfully with the least amount of help from the supervisor as possible. For example, guided discovery can be used to demonstrate knowledge a supervisee already has regarding a specific problem, then these strengths can be built upon in order to further draw out a supervisee's understanding of the situation. This is facilitated when a supervisor recognizes a supervisee's current abilities and provides guidance that allows the previously acquired skills to be further developed. Guided discovery is especially beneficial as it engages supervisees in the process of evaluating their emotions, behavior, thoughts, personal matters, and professional goals so that they can learn methods of improving their counseling practices (Todd & Freshwater, 1999). This approach is not about fixing problems related to a supervisee's style of counseling, but instead focuses on teaching a supervisee how to combine their knowledge with newly acquired skills in order to find solutions to challenges they face. More importantly, focusing on strengths as opposed to being judgmental or shaming a trainee helps reduce concerns and fear through confidence building. Furthermore, as supervisees learn from their experiences they will become more confident, begin to play a more proactive role in their clinical development, or even be encouraged to take risks such as applying novel counseling approaches that could greatly benefit their clients.

A supervisee should not be afraid to come to a supervisory meeting with mistakes to discuss, no matter what the magnitude. This is because a trainee should feel safe enough to display strengths as well as weaknesses during supervision, with the supervisor providing guided discovery in a non-judgmental manner, thereby ensuring that this will take place.

In addition to guided discovery, other strategies that facilitate progress include: reciprocal teaching, guided participation, cognitive apprenticeship, contingent learning, and assisted performance (Davies, 2000). Taken together, these types of methods should foster learning expertise, defined as the degree to which trainees continually try to refine their attitudes and counseling skills toward learning. These skills and attitudes include self-monitoring, practicing what is learned, and finding innovative ways to avoid plateaus in order to consistently move to the next stages of training (Bransford & Schwartz, 2009). Supervisors can help supervisees accomplish these tasks by using influence strategies that enhance empowerment.

Take for instance the following scenario that may occur during a supervisory meeting with supervisee Brad:

Supervisor: Hello Brad, I received your email regarding the difficult session you had with Jane (client) and I'm glad we are meeting to discuss. How can I help you best address this situation?

Brad: I don't know, I just think I'm not cut out for this profession.

Supervisor: Okay, can you explain a little more about why you think this profession isn't the right fit for you?

Brad: Well, I have been thinking a lot about this for the past couple of days and maybe she is right. Perhaps, I really don't know as much as I think about real life and I'm just a privileged graduate with a degree.

Supervisor: Those are some strong words. Is that what she said?

Brad: Yes, in a nutshell.

Supervisor: And have you doubted your choice to pursue this field since this happened?

Brad: It has been on my mind constantly for the last several days.

Supervisor: I can imagine this is difficult and I'm sorry you've been struggling with this issue. I also want to reassure you that we have all been challenged by a client at one point or another.

Brad: Really?

Supervisor: Yes, absolutely!

Brad: Counseling just seems to be so easy for my colleagues.

Supervisor: I'm sure that it may seem that way, but everyone who is an expert now was once a beginner at some point.

Brad: I just feel like I'm not prepared to handle such sensitive issues.

Supervisor: Can you tell me more about what you mean?

Brad: Well I just never had to deal with these kinds of issues before and I can't imagine not having supportive parents or being unemployed due to an alcohol addiction. I want to help my clients, but I don't know how to relate to them so I struggle to find the right words to say.

Supervisor: Okay, I can understand how hard it can be to address certain problems, but what bothered you the most about what she said?

Brad: It wasn't just what she said, but the way she said it. She was so critical that I froze and could not say anything.

Supervisor: I see. Based on what you've shared, there are several ways that we can address this. Together, we can try to see if you can remember the part of the conversation that set things in motion. We could also take a closer look at what aspects about this session trigger strong emotions for you. What are your thoughts regarding how we can proceed to best support you in this process.

In this case, the supervisor is trying to influence or encourage the supervisee to use reflection to reveal the reasons why the interaction with this particular client became problematic. This includes reflecting about the type of topics that were being discussed or the verbiage that was being used when the client began to demonstrate increased hostility or reactivity. Subsequently, the supervisor may also present which textbooks (e.g., theory, ethical standards) to review in such cases, followed by a professional opinion of how the supervisee could handle the situation he or she is facing. By providing both perspectives, the supervisor is offering choices, the very essence of empowerment in supervision. The ability to engage in self-reflection is also a key component of professional development.

Reflection helps supervisees explore their feelings and thoughts regarding positive or negative counseling experiences with clients as well as how their personal issues may be influencing their performance (Haynes et al., 2003). The application of reflection during a supervisory meeting also provides supervisees with a safe, supportive environment where they can take time to contemplate in a manner that would not be possible during a session with a client. Subsequently, a supervisee may begin to identify and understand emotions that certain sessions may evoke, and subsequently uncover ways to manage stress that is experienced while working with a client. However, reflection may also reveal ways to better relate to clients, especially when they display resistance or frustration during a counseling or therapy session. In the scenario of Brad that was previously presented, the supervisor subtly urged the supervisee to engage in reflection. Let's take a closer look at how this process helped Brad address his feelings about the situation:

Supervisor: What are your thoughts regarding how we can proceed?

Brad: I'm not really sure.

Supervisor: Well, give yourself a minute and ask yourself what about this situation was especially different from your other experiences?

Brad: Alright. (After a brief pause). It's just the way she stood up over me. It made me feel unsafe.

Supervisor: Okay, thank you for your honesty. Can I ask you to tell me more as to why you felt unsafe when she stood over you? Is there another possible reason why this caused you discomfort?

Brad: Wow, I hadn't thought about it before. Actually, whenever my parents disliked my opinion about a subject or disagreed with my career choice, they would stand up and argue with me. It seems like it was their way of making me feel smaller than them and even if I was already standing during an argument, I would still feel powerless when they started arguing with me.

Supervisor: That's interesting. Do you think your interaction with her triggered a similar response or emotion?

Brad: Yes, absolutely! I think it was even more difficult for me because my parents didn't want me to pursue a career in this field, even though they supported my education financially. I guess hearing her say that I don't know what I'm doing sounds like something my parents would say.

Supervisor: It sounds like we've found some new insight into your experience with Jane. I'm glad you felt comfortable enough to explore this with me.

This type of self-reflection may be enough to help the supervisee learn how to handle the same type of situation with clients in the future. For example, if the same client or another client were to become hostile and stand up during a session, instead of freezing the supervisee may ask questions such as "Did you realize that you got very upset and stood up when I asked you about this topic?" Another helpful question is "Can you tell me more about what part of our conversation caused you to become upset?" Therefore, reflection can help the supervisee develop professionally and subsequently provide better service and metaprocessing with clients. More specifically, becoming aware of personal strengths, weaknesses, vulnerabilities, and limits allows supervisees to make adjustments to their work performance in a natural, unforced, and instinctive manner. A supervisor who provides honesty and immediacy encourages reflection and accountability in the supervisee that applies to other areas of professional growth (e.g., exemplifying accountability while working with clients).

In addition to demonstrating the application of reflection, this scenario represents a commonly used supervision approach called *case consultation*, in which a supervisee describes major issues surrounding one or more cases to the supervisor (Haynes et al., 2003). Topics discussed may include: the reason why a client is seeking counseling; diagnostic methods; therapeutic approaches; progress notes regarding a case, and legal, ethical, and multicultural issues. Case consultation may be used to protect clients and promote their progress; to explore counseling skills; to encourage self-awareness and self-efficacy; and to help supervisees engage in self-reflection in a comfortable manner (Campbell, 2006). Accordingly, the ability to apply self-reflection may be enhanced through connectedness.

Connectedness occurs when an individual is actively involved with another individual or group and the involvement promotes a sense of well-being, comfort, and reduced anxiety (Hagerty et al., 1993). It is also described as a protective agent which prevents problems and aids in resolving inter-and intrapersonal concerns (Karcher, Davis, & Powell, 2002; Townsend & McWhirter, 2005). Connectedness is also defined as the act of building a supportive, professional relationship during training (Beidas et al., 2013). Interpersonal connectedness in particular encompasses attachment, bonding, companionship, friendship, and intimacy (Karcher et al.,

2002). Trainees have previously reported that connectedness was developed through individual interactions with training professionals (e.g., consultant) and group meetings (Beidas et al., 2013). They further indicated that the interpersonal connections reinforced their learning as well as the application of counseling practices. Therefore, supervisees who experience connectedness in their supervisory relationship may be better able to display reflection.

Interestingly, trainees mentioned that authenticity helped facilitate connectedness and further explained that training approaches they considered as authentic included those which allowed them to reflect upon challenging cases during their group meetings. This gave them opportunities to learn from their peers' clinical experiences as well. Responsiveness was another facilitator of connectedness that was described by the trainees as ways in which the training process was structured to respond to their stated needs for improved learning. This form of responsiveness helped the trainees feel more connected to the training professional and they were also more eager to learn and adopt the recommended practices (Beidas et al., 2013). Empowered connectedness, which occurs when an individual has a sense of feeling safe in the community and playing a meaningful role, can further facilitate this process as well (Kearney, 1998).

Indeed, one of the best experiences was described as a group supervisory meeting in which trainees exchanged ideas regarding practices that appeared to be working, those which did not, and suggestions about approaches to try. Furthermore, this type of shared experience and open reflection helps trainees recognize and reveal their own challenges in implementing certain practices. Most importantly, this process creates connectedness between trainees and supervisors as well as among trainees. Thusly, reflection and connectedness are interrelated concepts that support effective training and professional growth.

It is also important that supervisees feel comfortable enough in the supervisory relationship to advocate for the level of support that is needed (e.g., I need help preparing for court or I need to process emotions that came up in session for me today). A supervisor can help foster advocacy on the part of the supervisee by using lead statements and questions to best determine supervision goals and expectations for the supervisory relationship.

Examples of such questions and statements are as follows (Also see Appendix A):

- What goals would you like to accomplish during your supervision training?
- Let's discuss the counseling issues and topics that are currently the most pertinent to you.
- What type of guidelines should we establish regarding how we will work together?
- How can I help make the supervisory sessions feel like a safe place for you?
- How can we work together to help you become a more competent and confident helping professional?
- What types of experiences have you had in the past with various cultures?
- What do you feel like you need to learn in terms of multicultural issues when working with your clients?
- What do the ethical, professional, and legal standards dictate regarding this type of issue?
- Let's establish a plan for how we will address the evaluative feedback of your counseling performance.

- How could the evaluative sessions be most helpful for you?
- Can you tell me two or three different approaches to addressing this situation?
- What are some strategies you can suggest to resolve this issue?
- Which options best serve the goals and needs of the client?

This type of verbal exchange empowers supervisees to play an active role in their clinical training. It also helps supervisors determine where a supervisee currently is as well as what training methods and models will enable the supervisee to reach his or her full potential. As the supervisee gains experience and matures professionally, he or she will begin to display more self-direction and a proficient supervisor should be able to respond to such changes accordingly.

In addition to creating an environment that evokes connectedness, self-reflection, and autonomy, non-judgmental supervision fosters communication, enhanced learning, trust, and respect. Indeed, supervisees who have experienced this type of positive relationship reported that their supervisors were non-judgmental regarding their mistakes, demonstrated confidence and trust in their abilities, made them feel as if they were working with them instead of for them, and provided a safe supervision space (Ladany et al., 2013). It is important to remember that supervisees are going to make mistakes, but the manner in which a supervisor responds can support them in growth and learning. Trust and respect is also built through open discussion in which honest, empathetic, and friendly supervisors encourage supervisees to openly brainstorm their ideas about counseling with clients. Furthermore, when trust is established, a supervisee will begin to rely on his or her supervisor with a distinct sense of predictability. Clinical supervision is a time to teach and help guide new counselors to a greater understanding of clients and for them to conceptualize the needs of their clients. This is a fluid process, and during this period mistakes will be made. As a clinical supervisor, it is essential to come to the understanding that making errors is a part of the learning experience for supervisees, and to realize that a supervisor's response to mistakes influences whether or not those mistakes turn into a learning platform or a grievance for both parties.

Thusly, a supervisor whose tone is untrustworthy or judgmental may encounter resistance and mistrust from the supervisee as well as a hesitance to disclose pertinent information about personal anxieties or counseling sessions. In addition, criticism and shaming tend to lead to defensive behavior, especially if it causes individuals to doubt their competencies and abilities (NASW, 2013). Therefore, self-disclosure along with non-judgmental statements that empower supervisees and elicit trust, are much more effective forms of encouragement. Furthermore, even if a supervisee appears to have limited clinical experience, focusing initially on a singular strength and building upon it will be received more positively than exclusively emphasizing all of the areas that need to be improved. Understanding that mistakes on the supervisee's part are inevitable is essential toward promoting the learning process. Most importantly, establishing a supervisory relationship through trust and non-judgmental actions help supervisees build competence, which is an essential component of The Empowerment Model of Clinical Supervision.

Empowerment Elevated

Reality Perspective

Although The Empowerment Model strategies such as guided discovery are strength-based, new language is warranted as strengths are often overemphasized in the field of clinical supervision. As a supervisor, it is important to build upon a supervisee's strengths, but a more proficient level of counseling competence can be achieved by also focusing on areas that need to be improved upon. One approach to addressing weaknesses involves placing more emphasis on the *reality perspective* (Corey, 2012). This aspect of training may also be useful for supervisees who are reluctant to actively address their professional limitations. The application of the reality perspective entails developing specific and realistic goals of clinical training and then discussing how the training can be applied to work settings. This strategy provides a safe platform in which a supervisor can discuss observed limitations and the supervisee can also describe areas that he or she struggles with (e.g., anxiety about meeting new clients, avoiding transference).

It is essential that a supervisor does not tell a trainee what to change, but instead presents observations. The supervisee should subsequently be encouraged to examine how the limitations may influence counseling practices and whether his or her current approaches are meeting the counseling objectives. It is up to the supervisee to determine how well the working pattern is facilitating efficient services with clients and after completing this self-evaluation, the supervisee can decide to take significant steps to make any necessary changes. After a supervisee gains a better understanding of his or her vulnerabilities and certain patterns of behavior, a supervisor should encourage the development of a specific plan of action that should promote the desired changes. Sub-goals or simple weekly plans should be established initially and the supervisee should gradually get better at setting larger goals and making more realistic plans. That is, the reality perspective helps supervisees accept and understand that certain behaviors cannot be changed quickly due to forces within practice, but also challenges and supports them at becoming empowered to demonstrate more congruent counseling skills (Johns et al., 2009).

Collaboration

Collaborative 'We' statements can also help facilitate this process as *collaboration* places emphasis on sharing the responsibility of knowledge acquisition (Parlakian, 2001). This means that the supervisor and supervisee collaborate in order to promote learning. Both parties are aware of their knowledge about clients, the field, and oneself in the work setting and share a common goal of improving the supervisee's clinical skills. However, this type of collaboration does not exempt a supervisor from exercising authority or setting limits. The supervisor is still responsible for these tasks, but makes an added effort to encourage open dialogue about issues that affect the supervisee and the organization. This form of collaboration provides supervisors with an opportunity to learn from and teach supervisees. In addition, it allows supervisors to share in the decision-making and responsibility, thereby fostering leadership in the trainees. It also allows supervisees to express an interest in taking on new clinical challenges and tasks, as well as to exercise some control over the conditions of their clinical training.

In a collaborative supervisory relationship, both the supervisor and supervisee clearly understand each other's expectations as this partnership is jointly developed and agreed upon at the initiation of the clinical training. The collaborative relationship should also be built on safety and trust as this creates a working environment in which difficult topics can be discussed without the fear of feeling judged, shamed, or ridiculed. Therefore, open communication is the key to true collaboration.

Interestingly, The Empowerment Model demonstrates the different layers of collaboration that a supervisor may have with a supervisee. For instance, a supervisor can teach the supervisee new counseling approaches as well as how to combine such techniques with previous knowledge. However, the supervisee is also empowered to use the learning experiences as opportunities to teach him- or herself how to self-supervise. In doing so, both parties are collaborating in order to facilitate professional development. There may also be research-related collaboration in which a supervisor may encourage participation on the supervisee's part. Collaboration may even take place at the consultant level where the supervisee may offer professional advice to a fellow trainee and still request consultation from a supervisor in order to ensure that appropriate advice was provided. In this case, both parties would be displaying a collaborative effort to assist other supervisees. Therefore, collaboration may be useful at all levels of clinical training.

Self-Care

Another important aspect of The Empowerment Model of Clinical Supervision is *self-care*. In the helping professional field, counselors focus most of their attention, energy, and time toward caring for other people, but it is also imperative that they take proper care of themselves (Norcross & Guy, 2007). Therefore, increasing importance is being placed on counselor self-care to prevent vicarious traumatization and burnout. Self-care also helps improve work performance, and adhering to self-care guidelines is an ethical imperative that counselors should embrace (Norcross & Guy, 2007). This means that self-care is a key topic that supervisors should discuss with supervisees, especially if it is discovered that a supervisee's inadequate self-care is negatively affecting his or her ability to provide clients with beneficial services. Research even indicates that effective clinical supervision positively influences reported levels of burnout in trainees (Edwards et al., 2006).

Although self-care encompasses factors such as maintaining a proper diet and getting adequate amounts of rest, it also entails having supervision time set aside to vent frustrations and emotions related to counseling. Thusly, quality supervision time is an essential part of a supervisee's self-care routine. More importantly, it is imperative that a supervisee feels safe enough to reveal such emotions regarding supervision without fear of experiencing any form of retribution. This is because being able to share experiences with a trusted supervisor can give the supervisee strength, hope, and an optimistic perspective that can be very useful. Indeed, healthier supervisees will become more effective counselors who are better prepared for their jobs. Overall, self-care allows professionals to be more mentally present and subsequently more efficient, which is one of the primary goals of clinical supervision.

There are a number of ways that self-care strategies can be introduced without crossing into therapy. However, gaining an understanding of a supervisee's situation in life before a self-care regimen is recommended is of the utmost importance. Furthermore, for supervisees who display resistance, it may be useful to explain that self-care for helping professionals is directly linked to quality of service (Norcross & Guy, 2007). Once a supervisee is in agreement, a self-care plan should be developed and implemented.

According to the National Institute for Occupational Safety and Health, the following components are essential for a self-care plan (NIOSH, 2008):

- Finding the proper balance between family, work, and a personal life
- Having a support system of coworkers and/or friends
- Maintaining a positive and relaxed outlook on life

Supervisors can share this basic framework with supervisees, especially when they begin to struggle with keeping their commitments to self-care. This information is useful because when these three components are presented during a supervisory session for example, a trainee can usually determine which of these areas need the most attention. For example, a supervisee who is reconsidering the decision to continue training in this field may need additional support from friends and colleagues. There may be deficits in all three areas, but in this case the supervisor may still want to emphasize the importance of seeking an increased level of support. A supervisor can also employ professional guidance to help a supervisee amplify the specific component of self-care that will best facilitate optimal mental health. We've included a wellness plan in this book under Appendix C for both supervisee and client use.

The self-care aspect emphasizes the importance of focusing on both the *'individual self'* as well as the *'clinician self'*. The individual self refers to all personal matters outside the realm of counseling. This includes family life, social life, personal problems, interests, hobbies, physical health, and emotional well-being. Taking the steps that are necessary to maintain the health of the individual self helps ensure that professionalism will be exemplified at the workplace. However, the clinician self is as much of an attribute for the supervisee as any other clinical skill and the acknowledgment of self-issues in clinical supervision is the key to providing high quality counseling services that demonstrate genuine concern for the clients (Edwards et al., 2006; NIOSH, 2008; Norcross & Guy, 2007). Conversely, unaddressed clinician self-issues may result in unprofessional or unhelpful coping strategies as well as rigid clinical boundaries that can cause counselors to become ineffective. This can have damaging consequences for both the client and the counselor. That is, individual counselors may experience burnout or other risk factors that may overflow into clinical work and have negative impacts on their clients. Therefore, it is the responsibility of the organization and especially the supervisor to care for supervisees who have worked with traumatized clients to ensure that they are able to successfully separate work life and their personal life.

On the next page is an example of a dialogue between a supervisor and supervisee regarding self-care:

Supervisor: Brad, you've been growing a lot through this process of working with diverse, trauma clients and I'm curious how you are managing self-care during this time in your career.

Brad: It's hard to fit it all in with clients, paperwork, and trying to get my hours for licensure.

Supervisor: Can you talk with me further on what kinds of activities or elements you are tracking when defining self-care?

Brad: I guess I would say I'm trying to make sure to eat several times a day and get 7-9 hours sleep. I don't have a lot of time to socialize but those pieces I feel I can control.

Supervisor: I appreciate your honesty and efforts! As part of our meeting today, I want to introduce you to a Wellness Plan, which is a tool to track self-care and burnout. It can also be used with your clients to support their self-care and needs. Would this tool be helpful to you?

Brad: Absolutely. I don't want to burn out before I'm even fully in my career so I'd be curious to see what else it can tell me about myself and maybe help me identify what self-care could mean to me.

Accordingly, if it is discovered during a supervisory session that a supervisee is dealing with issues that require therapy or counseling, the supervisor should make a referral for support. More specifically, the supervisee should be provided with the contact details of an appropriate referral source or even an employee assistance program. Clinical supervision is not counseling or therapy, and although it is important for a supervisor to be aware of how personal situations in life may influence work performance, it is not the role of the supervisor to provide counseling for issues that are not directly related to working with clients in counseling settings. It is, however, imperative that a supervisor make a referral for support if it becomes necessary as this helps supervisees maintain optimal emotional health for the clinician self as well as the individual self. In doing so, a supervisor adheres to the dual role of supervision, which is to: establish and maintain the supervisee's competent, professional well-being and functioning while safeguarding client services.

Care of the clinician self and individual self involves setting up specific supervisory sessions that provide:

- A safe place to reflect, debrief, and discuss emotional containment

- An environment to process and address personal reactions
- A place to discuss joy, successful sessions, and inspiration
- Opportunities to contemplate the separation of professional reactions from personal reactions
- An opportunity for a supervisor to make a referral for therapy when responses to trauma cannot be addressed through supervision.

Overall, it becomes the responsibility of the supervisor to help a supervisee prioritize self-care time, which includes allotting a certain amount of time (e.g., 3 or more hours a week) to self-care.

In The Empowerment Model, supervisors have a wide range of responsibilities, but there are four main focus areas of clinical counseling that should be emphasized during training; these are:

- cognitive counseling skills
- counseling performance skills
- self-awareness
- and professional behavior

Cognitive counseling skills involve the specific aspects of counseling a supervisee thinks about before, during, and after a session with a client. This encompasses case conceptualization which is facilitated through the recognition of themes and patterns, thought processes throughout a session, observing what is happening and what a client needs, deciding how to respond or offer intervention, and assessing personal efforts.

Counseling performance skills pertain to a supervisee's actions during a session such as theoretically based approaches (e.g., dream analysis, circular questioning), basic and advanced helping (e.g., confrontation immediacy, empathetic responding), issue-specific skills (e.g., suicide assessment), and procedural skills (e.g., beginning and ending a session).

Self-awareness refers to a supervisee's ability to identify personal beliefs, motivations, emotions, and issues that may affect his or her case conceptualization skills as well as behavior during sessions. This also includes being aware of personal history as this can also influence a supervisee's perceptions, cause overly positive or negative views of a client, lead to the identification with or distance from a client, or cloud overall objectivity.

Professional behaviors entail displaying appropriate on-site conduct (e.g., following protocols for documentation and emergency situations, punctuality, attendance) and adhering to legal, professional, and ethical guidelines.

Figure 1.1 The Empowerment Model of Clinical Supervision

Each of these focus areas can be addressed through the various roles of a supervisor, which include: supervisor (self), counselor, educator/teacher, researcher, consultant, and colleague. Although clinical counseling supervisors do not actually hold a position in each one of these professions, they are able to apply their knowledge and skills in relation to each role.

Revisiting our model, the role of the **supervisor** is distinct in that clinical supervisors are primarily skill focused and instructional, although they also provide the direction, explanation, structure, modeling, encouragement, and support that is needed by novice trainees. These factors are important for building rapport and although this role implies that the supervisor is the authority figure, a collaborative as opposed to an authoritarian relationship is generally more productive in terms of clinical training (Borders & Brown, 2005). Furthermore, supervisors can foster learning by drawing from their past experiences, which may include business matters such as establishing a supervision training and/or counseling contract, computer systems (e.g., e-technology services), or even aspects of theology such as the relevance of spirituality, morality, etc., that govern ethical decision making.

Supervisees are often eager to learn how to become more competent counselors and they usually fear what they may uncover about themselves. A supervisor's skills enable them to understand that this is a normal dynamic that has to be addressed in order for a supervisee to develop his or her true potential as a counselor. It is also the role of the supervisor to present interventions that help supervisees identify and surmount fears which are inherent to professional growth and development. This means that addressing a supervisee's personal issues is acceptable, but the focus should involve discussing how to handle such issues in a manner that does not interfere with counseling a client or prevent a decision regarding a potential resolution from being made. At times this distinction is unclear as are the ethical implications for crossing over into the counselor role.

The *counselor* role entails establishing a working relationship with the supervisee. Facilitative skills such as primary empathy, warmth, concreteness, and genuineness are also fostered through this relationship, as well as challenging skills which include confrontation, advanced empathy, immediacy, and self-disclosure. Additional aspects of the counselor role involve promoting supervisee self-exploration, enhancing knowledge of counseling theories and interpersonal dynamics, heightening a supervisee's ability to conduct intake and closure sessions, and improving the ability to recognize when to make referrals.

An essential role that the counselor (supervisor) plays is fostering supervisees' expertise with specific clients and issues (e.g., substance abuse, anxiety, suicide). When acting as a counselor, the supervisor also works with supervisees on skills that are needed to respond to a client's challenges in an empathetic manner. This includes, for example, positively reframing a client's challenging behavior as guarded or an act of self-protection. It may also become necessary to help a supervisee identify resistive feelings in response to a client's arduous conduct and to further explore his or her emotions in relation to counseling such as having to break confidentiality to discuss certain aspects of the case. However, it is important to remember that although counseling skills are being applied during clinical training, a supervisor is not a supervisee's counselor. Any supervisee who needs counseling intervention should be given an appropriate referral by the clinical supervisor.

The **teacher** role entails assisting supervisees to develop new counseling skills and knowledge by identifying learning styles and needs, determining strengths and areas of weakness, conferring knowledge for professional growth and practical use, and promoting self-awareness (Borders & Brown, 2005). The teaching role also involves establishing learning goals and objectives, developing instructional strategies that facilitate learning, and presenting material in both a didactic and experimental manner. The experimental approach to teaching refers to exploring different strategies (e.g., guided discovery, scaffolded instruction, reciprocal teaching, etc.) that appear to be best suited for each supervisee. For example, counseling performance skills that can be taught in this setting include learning how to apply a paradoxical intervention, positive reframing, or the gestalt two-chair technique as well as practicing confrontation skills (Borders & Brown, 2005).

In addition to counseling performance skills, emphasis is placed on cognitive counseling skills, self-awareness, and professional behaviors. For example, a new supervisee may not have extensive experience with counseling clients who have a substance abuse disorder. In such cases, the teacher (supervisor) can encourage the supervisee to consider how a family history of substance abuse may influence a client's behavior as this exemplifies the application of cognitive skills. The teacher can also promote self-awareness by explaining how personal reactions to a client's case are informative about the client's self-presentation. Accordingly, professional behavior is encouraged by discussing the ethical standards that apply to this type of case as well as the importance of considering the client's welfare when making decisions about therapeutic interventions. Subsequently, the teaching role of supervision helps supervisees understand the rationale for applying specific interventions, evaluates a supervisee's learning, and provides constructive feedback regarding counseling services. In doing so, a supervisor exemplifies the role of a teacher, trainer, and professional role model (Milne & Reiser, 2017).

There is also the role of *researcher* which entails making reliable and accurate observations of both the supervisees and their clients. However, more specific responsibilities involve developing testable hypotheses (e.g., Would the two-chair technique be an effective intervention for supervision? Is the supervisee repeatedly avoiding confrontation?), gathering appropriate data, and evaluating the hypotheses based on collected data. As a researcher, a supervisor must also be able to incorporate any new data that is obtained into future research as well as restate and retest additional hypotheses. The identification of confounding variables that may have interaction effects on cases such as a supervisee's personal issues, is also one of the responsibilities of the researcher. Furthermore, a competent researcher demonstrates the ability to critically examine and incorporate beneficial findings of research into supervision as this promotes the advancement of various clinical areas such as counseling intervention, assessment, counselor-client dynamics, supervision interaction, etc.

A supervisor is also a ***consultant*** who objectively assesses the current skills of supervisees and counsels them about their job performance. In addition, the role of a consultant entails encouraging supervisees to make their own choices, to take responsibility for decisions regarding client services, and to review, monitor, and provide consultation about cases. This includes offering alternative case conceptualizations and/or interventions as well as engaging in the oversight of supervisee counseling services to achieve goals that were mutually agreed upon. In doing so, the consultation facilitates the brainstorming of options and solutions, as well as rapport that leads to a more collegial, peer-like relationship with the supervisee (Bernard & Goodyear, 2004).

Most importantly, a supervisor who is exemplifying the role of a consultant functions as a professional gatekeeper for the discipline and organization. An important example of gatekeeping is recognizing supervisee impairments that could affect the welfare of the clients and taking the steps that are necessary to address the observed limitations. Similarly, consultation in supervision may encompass issues such as working on understanding why a particular intervention was not successful with a client or responding to a supervisee's negative emotions toward a client. In such cases, it is important that the consulting supervisor responds to the supervisee's feelings by explaining that this is an ethical situation and subsequently presenting options for responding to the client in a professional manner. When supervisees reach this developmental level, they are typically capable of identifying the focus area for supervision and will request a supervisor's help or consultation with more sophisticated or subtle areas such as a confusing paradox, an unexpected internal reaction to a client, or understanding an impasse. However, the consultant role is described as the least distinct because it is an underlying component of the other roles, but especially the supervisor's. An important distinction that must be made is the difference in liability for a consultant and a supervisor. More specifically, a consultant does not typically have the same level of responsibility or liability as a supervisor as this role mostly entails providing advice or feedback, without having to know personal information about the clients (Polychronis & Brown, 2016). Conversely, a clinical supervisor is responsible and legally liable for all of the actions and services of their supervisees including:

- Knowing key details regarding clients' cases
- Assisting supervisees with interventions
- Monitoring the progress of supervisees' clients
- Managing ethical issues that supervisees experience
- Improving the overall quality of care for the supervisees' clients

Therefore, when referring to the role of a consultant in the realm of clinical supervision, the supervisor is still fully responsible for treatment even if the supervisor does not meet a supervisee's clients in person. Furthermore, each state has its own regulations regarding legal liability (Polychronis & Brown, 2016).

It is important to understand this distinction because one of the primary goals of counseling training is for the supervisee to gradually move away from clinical supervision and dependency to self-supervision and autonomy. When this is achieved, the supervisor's role becomes that of a *colleague*. This is a supportive role as supervisory skills are used to motivate, relate to, and understand a supervisee. Furthermore, a supervisor promotes morale building and suggests various clinical approaches only when asked to, at this stage of clinical supervision. For entry-level counselors there is a progressive shift from conditional reliance on the supervisor, which is a period of tension and confusion, to apprehensions and anxiety about performance, followed by realistic confidence. The final stage, in which the counselor becomes a colleague, involves integration and expertise, however collegial support is still critical at this stage.

More importantly, supervisors become more engaged in helping supervisees contemplate their decisions instead of guiding and training them. They also discontinue approaches such as scaffolded instruction and move away from the one-on-one supervision the supervisee previously needed to stay in role, as it assumes that supervisees will now be able to efficiently identify issues that need to be addressed during sessions. Thusly, the counselor becomes the leader and the language that was used during training changes in order to promote individualized decision-making.

The role of a colleague also involves demonstrating respect as the supervisee, who is now a colleague, is moving from external to internal evaluation and feedback. In doing so, the colleague (supervisee) is exemplifying a new-found professional identity, is the main individual who makes counseling-related choices and is a leader in her or her own right. The supervisor's role also shifts to a colleague who provides ongoing support, especially with the new leader's (supervisee's) evolving professional identity. This is because a supervisee who reaches the level of colleague and leader may develop apprehensions about the new social roles. That is, the implications for this role shift include: different priorities such as working full-time in a specific field (e.g., family therapy), addressing new questions (e.g., Am I competent with online-therapy?), and facing new challenges (e.g., training to be a clinical or administrative supervisor). An administrative supervisor has additional training, requirements, responsibilities, and preferences related to the oversight of entry-level counselors. This means that the collegial relationship should remain focused on the supervisee who has become a colleague and leader, as this is still a critical developmental stage in the supervisee's professional career.

Determining Clinical Roles

The appropriate determination and performance in each of the above roles promotes mastery of cognitive counseling skills, counseling performance skills, self-awareness, and professional behavior. Accordingly, the educator/teacher, counselor, researcher, and consultant roles are sequenced throughout a supervisee's career, although more focus is placed on counseling performance skills during the early phases, while self-awareness and cognitive counseling skills are given more attention in the middle and later phases. This structure provides an instructive, comprehensive framework for effective clinical supervision, and a periodic assessment of supervisee developmental level demonstrates whether a supervisee is progressing or struggling. There are three stages which are assessed: stability or stagnation (stage 1); confusion (stage 2); and integration (stage 3). The integration stage is reached when each of the following criteria are mastered:

- Competence – expertise in counseling skills and techniques as well as displaying the ability to take appropriate action when it becomes necessary.
- Emotional Awareness – Understanding how personality and personal issues may influence counseling performance, being able to differentiate feelings, and demonstrating the capacity to use emotions/reactions diagnostically.
- Autonomy – Being able to make independent decisions or choices, displaying self-directedness to the appropriate degree, and having a strong sense of self.
- Identity – Demonstrating theoretical consistency, the integration of counseling concepts, and a sense of self as a counselor.

- Respect for Individual Differences – Making an active effort to display deep respect and understanding for colleagues and clients as well as an appreciation of differences.

- Purpose and Direction – Demonstrates expertise with formulating treatment plans, appropriate short- or long-term goals, and mapping out a client's progress.

- Personal Motivation – Understands the meaning of personal drives, reward satisfaction, and the complex, evolving nature of personal motivation.

- Professional Ethics – Encompasses legal issues, values, and professional standards as well as the integration of these factors into ongoing counseling.

Accordingly, effective clinical supervision ensures that supervisees will acquire the knowledge and skills that will allow them to gradually draw upon the characteristics of a supervisor, counselor, consultant, teacher, researcher, and colleague throughout their clinical career.

Back to Basics Using The Empowerment Model

Focus of Boundaries in Clinical Supervision

The American Counseling Association (ACA) Code of Ethics, section *C.2.a Boundaries of Competence*, states that (ACA, 2014):

> Counselors practice only within the boundaries of their competence, based on their education, training, supervised experience, state and national professional credentials, and appropriate professional experience. Whereas multicultural counseling competency is required across all counseling specialties, counselors gain knowledge, personal awareness, sensitivity, dispositions, and skills pertinent to being a culturally competent counselor in working with a diverse client population.

Accordingly, the supervisory relationship is an optimal platform through which supervisees can gain an understanding of boundaries in clinical supervision.

Boundary issues that are directly related to supervision include (Norcross, 2011):

- violating professional responsibilities to a supervisee
- dealing with unethical or incompetent behavior
- crossing ethical, legal, or professional violations

The same boundaries that are pertinent to supervision can be paralleled in a counseling setting. The following vignettes reflect issues that supervisees may face and supervisors should be ready to address:

In-Home Therapy "I'm not hungry."

Sally, a Marriage and Family Therapist, is staffing her case of the Smith family who she sees weekly in their home for family therapy. Sally expresses some concern of boundaries due to the family consistently offering her food when she is in their home and when sessions overlap with after school snack or dinner time. She expresses worry of damaging rapport by refusing food, but also expresses concern in not wanting to be seen as favoring the family due to her role in assessing reunification with their open Department of Human Services (DHS) case.

Q: What role from The Empowerment Model would you start with to support your supervisee?

Q: What questions would you ask about the family system, ethnicity, race, and heritage?

Q: How would you model good boundaries so that your supervisee has confidence in setting healthy boundaries with her clients?

Taking Gifts from Clients "Christmas cheer!"

Nico, a new grad counselor, calls you to share that his client Sandra is reporting she's buying him a gift for Christmas for helping her turn her life around. Nico expresses to you as his supervisor that he is both appreciative and nervous due to the ethical guidelines around gifts.

Q: What role from The Empowerment Model would you start with to support your supervisee?

Q: How do you explore Nico's thoughts to develop an appropriate plan of action?

Q: What questions could you ask about client background that could relate to gift giving?

Attraction with Clients "Let's get coffee."

Clarice, a recently licensed professional counselor, comes to you for supervision. She is sitting in your office with her head down, you can barely hear her speak and she won't look you in the eye. Clarice is expressing embarrassment that she didn't redirect Terrence, her client, when he asked her on a date suddenly at the end of their intake appointment.

Q: What role from The Empowerment Model would you start with to support your supervisee?
Q: How can you best address Clarice's discomfort?
Q: How would you encourage Clarice to address her concerns with the client in therapeutic ways?

Sexual Contact "A deeper connection."

Stephen, a Psychologist, appears defensive and begins fidgeting when you bring up a question of boundaries between Stephen and his client Alejandra. You've been contacted by Alejandra's spouse, who reports that he suspects Stephen and his wife are engaging in a sexual relationship.

Q: What role from the Empowerment Model would you start with to support your supervisee?

Q: How do you explore this allegation with Stephen?

Q: What steps need to be taken by you as the Supervisor?

Bartering "It will help us both."

Abigale, a Master's level Social Worker, is calling for support on addressing her client John's request to exchange yard work for therapy sessions due to John's financial limitations this month.

Q: What role from The Empowerment Model would you start with to support your supervisee?

Q: How do you explore this offer from the client with Abigale including the short-term and long-term effects?

Q: What ideas could be generated with Abigale to best serve John?

The following vignettes reflect common challenges that are faced in community mental health programs:

Confidentiality:

Community Contact "I need some milk."

Tommy is a young dad who frequents the grocery store around the corner from his counselor Jordan's office. Jordan is grabbing lunch when he runs into Tommy at the store. Jordan reports feeling uncomfortable seeing his client outside of the office and is looking for guidance on how to navigate the unplanned community contact.

Q: What should you advise Jordan to do?
Q: How can you support Jordan in addressing community contact with Tommy in a future session?

Secondary Referrals "A friend of a friend."

Daphne, a Licensed Clinical Social Worker, receives a call for a referral by Deja who reports she is the sister of Daphne's client and is seeking her own referral for a mental health professional.

Q: How should Daphne respond?
Q: What confidentiality concerns are present?

Colleague Referrals "I cannot confirm or deny."

Roger is a case manager for Rocky Creek Primary Care, calling to confirm his client connected and set up an intake with Miranda, a Psychologist in a private practice.

Q: How should Miranda respond?
Q: What confidentiality concerns are present?

Release of Information (ROI) Revoked and Third-Party Contact "Your records are required."

Armand is calling from a life insurance company stating he has a release to speak with Veronica, a Master's level therapist providing trauma services to Clementine, in order to approve her request for a life insurance policy. Veronica did not confirm or deny working with the client and asks to call Armand back. Veronica calls you for support, stating her client Clementine did not sign a release or give permission to speak with Armand. Veronica had called Clementine to explore what was needed and Clementine declined giving verbal or written permission to return Armand's calls.

Q: How should Veronica respond to her lack of release and the possibility of Armand's continued return calls?
Q: How do you support your supervisee in working with her client to make a release a possibility to support continuity of care?

Team Goals/Outcomes & Collaboration
"There are so many agendas."

Oliver, a Masters-level therapist, has been assigned to provide family therapy to support active and appropriate parenting between parents recently engaged in sobriety, and their 4-year-old child who has been placed with a relative. While reviewing an email request from the assigned caseworker, he recognizes that one of the goals from DHS is for the child to remain with the relative rather than reunification. Since Oliver's role is in support of reunification, he comes to you feeling frustrated with the lack of progress in the case.

Q: What role from The Empowerment Model would you start with to support your supervisee?

Q: How would you support Oliver in reflection around his frustration?

Q: What can be identified to support Oliver's role of collaboration with DHS?

Frequency of Supervision "I need to reschedule."

Ellie, a recent grad counselor has texted your work cell again to share she's caught up with clients and can't attend supervision. This is the second time in two weeks that she's cancelled at the last minute.

Q: What role from The Empowerment Model would you start with to support your supervisee?

Q: What questions would you ask about engaging in supervision?

Q: How would you model positive communication for your supervisee to have confidence in setting healthy communication and boundaries with her clients?

Competence "It feels like too many miles."

Eduardo, an addictions counselor, agrees to take on a new client in the neighboring city for home-based therapy. After completing the intake, he comes back to supervision and states he doesn't want to drive that far every week.

Q: What role from The Empowerment Model would you start with to support your supervisee?
Q: How will you explore Eduardo's perspective in neutral and supportive ways?
Q: What steps need to be taken to address the concern of client abandonment?

Bias "I don't think he will engage anyways."

Lexie, a new grad therapist is working with her first mandatory client, a teen boy named Julian. She comes to supervision expressing frustration that he won't engage with her in sessions and that she has tried various activities to build rapport. Lexie states he needs to cooperate or he will have a negative report to his probation officer.

Q: What role from The Empowerment Model would you start with to support your supervisee?
Q: How would you explore cultural and trauma factors in building rapport between Lexie and her teen client?

Q: How might you explore Lexie's expectations of mandatory clients in order to support her with professional growth and progress?

Expectations *"She won't talk to me."*

Charlie, a therapist candidate, reports he's concerned with the lack of progress with his soft-spoken client Ginger. Charlie shares it's been two months and she still won't open up about her former abusive relationship.

Q: What role from The Empowerment Model would you start with to support your supervisee?
Q: What questions would you ask about the structure of Charlie's sessions with Ginger?
Q: How would you evaluate the expectations Charlie has set for himself in working with his client?

Ethics and Dual Roles

Supervisors help promote ethical decision-making by discussing and modeling the principles, regulations, and values that are inherent to the organization as well as the manner in which challenging issues can be effectively addressed. In addition, a supervisory meeting provides a good opportunity to discuss the benefits and potential repercussions of certain actions. This important conversation should encourage the exploration of responses to arduous issues that can best achieve justice, respect, and fairness for all parties involved. Furthermore, if a supervisee makes an ethical mistake, it should promptly be addressed, and with the supervisor's assistance, both parties should work toward ameliorating the damage and identifying strategies to prevent similar mistakes from being made in the future. However, the degree of the violation may also necessitate a report being sent to the licensing board, especially if this is required by the jurisdiction.

A serious ethical violation involves entering a familial or romantic relationship with a supervisee. This type of relationship needs to be avoided as it causes a role conflict that completely undermines the goal of clinical supervision. If, however, a supervisor notices a potential boundary violation with a supervisee, it should be acknowledged in a timely manner, assessed to determine how the boundary violation has influenced supervision, and the conflict should be resolved. Although the supervisory relationship is of a professional nature, the supervisor is usually in the position of power in comparison to the supervisee. Therefore, in order to avoid conflicts of interest and boundary problems, an ethical supervisor respects this level of power and uses his or her authority to demonstrate accountability and ensure that clients are protected. In addition, supervisors who work with more than one supervisee must structure the supervision training to each individual's abilities and needs. Additionally, supervisors must also be sure to find the right balance of consistency and fairness when working with multiple supervisees.

An additional ethical consideration is that a supervisor must focus on the goals of clinical supervision and the dynamics of the supervisory relationship in order to avoid providing supervisees with applied psychotherapy services. If this occurs, it means a supervisor has crossed over into the role of a personal counselor and this contradicts the aims of supervision. A means of staying within the boundaries of the supervisory relationship involves being discreet in terms of sharing personal information and not allowing self-disclosure to become the focus of a meeting. Any personal information that is disclosed should support the supervision objectives. Furthermore, the rationale behind comments that are made should be thoroughly explained to help supervisees understand how to apply the information in counseling settings. Similarly, there are times where a clinical supervisor may react to a supervisee in a way a counselor would react to a client. The use of counseling skills is appropriate when supervisees are being encouraged to demonstrate self-awareness in order to positively influence professional functioning. It is, however, important to watch for signs of the relationship becoming more therapeutic than supervisory. The initial supervision meeting is a good opportunity to explain to supervisees that counseling will not be provided as this helps prevent boundary problems.

The ACA Code of Ethics, section *F.3.a Extending Conventional Supervisory Relationships*, states that (ACA, 2014):

> Counseling supervisors clearly define and maintain ethical professional, personal, and social relationships with their supervisees. Supervisors consider the risks and benefits of extending current supervisory relationships in any form beyond conventional parameters. In extending these boundaries, supervisors take appropriate professional precautions to ensure that judgment is not impaired and that no harm occurs.

Although this statement makes reference to boundary precautions that should be taken, dual relationships are often the underlying factor for most ethics-related boundary issues.

There are three common types of dual roles: therapeutic, social, and sexual (Borders & Brown, 2005). A dual relationship arises when an association other than one which is professional develops. This can occur between a client and a supervisee or a supervisor and a supervisee (e.g., a supervisee has a business the supervisor would like to receive services from) (Reamer, 2003). The supervisor is responsible for paying close attention to dual roles with supervisees and recognizing when boundaries are potentially being crossed between a supervisee and a client. It is hard, however, for supervisors to avoid overlapping social roles as they may, for example, teach a supervisee in class or serve as an academic advisor. The familiarity of the supervision meetings may also promote a personal friendship with supervisees that may create a potentially troublesome dual relationship. However, if the differences between these roles are clearly explained, conflicts associated with multiple roles can typically be prevented.

The following is a list of several cues to potential boundary issues:

- Therapizing a supervisee, which is described as one of the most problematic boundary violations that occurs when a supervisor abuses his or her position by exerting condescension or undue power.
- Developing strong feelings toward a supervisee or client and engaging in inconsistent boundaries to extend meetings. Extending a session is only justified if the client/supervisee needs more time to discuss counseling-related topics or to address a crisis. If professional and personal caring begins to

merge, the opposing party's feelings need to be redirected to allow boundaries to be reinforced or reinstated.

- Sexual attraction, which may in some cases develop due to sharing similar values, hobbies, and interests. If the attraction leads to seductive behavior, sexual fantasies, physical contact, etc., a meeting should be dedicated to avoiding further conflict or relinquishing the working relationship with referral to another professional.

- An inappropriate conversation that arises during a car pool between a supervisor and a supervisee. This is characterized as a discussion that gradually shifts from professional to informal due to the private environment of the vehicle. If this occurs, the supervisor should explain the difference between applied psychotherapy services and case management, which encourages the exploration of role confusion.

- Providing home phone or cell numbers, as this may result in calls after hours. If a number is exchanged, the purpose of the after-hour calls as well as the counselor/client or supervisor/supervisee role should be clarified.

- Giving a gift to or accepting gifts from a client/supervisee. Gift giving necessitates the exploration of what the gift means and why the perception of the working relationship has changed.

- Over-identifying, overdoing, or overprotecting, which is characterized by doing too much or additional signs of enmeshment. This type of behavior needs to be redirected.

- In-home boundary problems as family services may lead to ambivalent situations that a supervisor should explore with a supervisee to establish factors that contributed to the change in the professional relationship.

- Touching, as this can quickly become risky behavior that may be misinterpreted by a supervisee/client. The rules and repercussions of physical contact should be established and agreed upon by both parties.

- Sales of goods, loans, or bartering (e.g., paying for services from a supervisee or client). Clear, unambiguous procedures, guidelines, and policies should be established to prevent this type of dual relationship from occurring.

Each of these types of boundary issues should be quickly addressed and rectified if they occur. This is because even inadvertent violations of boundaries can cause a supervisee or a client harm. Therefore, small indiscretions should not be ignored as they can become bigger concerns. Just as counselors establish written contracts for their clients, supervisors may want to consider having a supervisee sign a weekly/bi-weekly supervision contract (see Appendix B) that makes all expectations clear and explains that the contract provides permission for a routine evaluation of potential boundary issues.

Alcohol Use "I'm just sleepy."

Ritchie, a social worker, calls you between supervision meetings to share an encounter with his most recent family therapy session with The Carters. Ritchie discloses that he felt Mr. Carter was under the influence of a substance during the family therapy session due to slurring his words, leaning back to close his eyes, and dozing off occasionally while the family therapy session was taking place. Ritchie shares that he asked Mr. Carter privately if he was under the influence, which Mr. Carter denied, but Ritchie felt he smelled alcohol on his breath and wonders what he needs to share with the Human Services case manager assigned to the family.

Q: What role from The Empowerment Model would you start with to support your supervisee?
Q: What elements of the family therapy session need to be documented for the client file as well as the case manager?
Q: How would you support your supervisee in brainstorming engagement of the client around alcohol compliance and ethical considerations?

Mandatory Reporting: Documentation needs "She's on edge."

Conrad, a new graduate therapist is providing supervised visitation between grandma Estrella and her three grandchildren. Conrad is seeking support from you due to DHS demands for more information in his reports, and pushback from Estrella, who is concerned about the details of her visits being recorded with her grandchildren.

Q: What role from The Empowerment Model would you start with to support your supervisee?

Q: How can you support Conrad in his documentation to comply with DHS?

Q: What strategies can support Conrad in building rapport and trust with Estrella in the visitations?

Mandatory Reporting: Documentation needs "She's on edge."

Conrad, a new graduate therapist is providing supervised visitation between grandma Estrella and her three grandchildren. Conrad is seeking support from you due to DHS demands for more information in his reports, and pushback from Estrella, who is concerned about the details of her visits being recorded with her grandchildren.

Q: What role from The Empowerment Model would you start with to support your supervisee?

Q: How can you support Conrad in his documentation to comply with DHS?

Q: What strategies can support Conrad in building rapport and trust with Estrella in the visitations?

Crisis Support

Crises cannot be avoided within the helping professional field, but this may be a new and distressing situation for some supervisees. Therefore, supervisors must establish procedures that allow supervisees to contact them, or other professionals who may be on-call in their absence, in the event of a crisis. However, there must be a clearly delineated boundary regarding what is deemed as a counseling-related crisis. More specifically, before any form of contact information is provided both parties should agree upon the description of crises that warrant the assistance of a supervisor. These types of events include:

- A client reporting that he or she was the victim of a violent crime or abuse.
- A client who is expressing suicidal ideations or an imminent suicide attempt.
- A life-changing event (e.g., hurricane destruction, death in the family) that causes a client to relapse or experience a harmful mental state.

Even though supervisees should have a supervisor's contact information for crisis support, they should still be made aware of emergency services that they can refer clients to such as mobile crisis units, crisis hotlines, victim support groups, or crisis centers. Self-supervision is one of the main objectives of clinical training, thusly a supervisee needs to gradually learn how to address crises independently. Furthermore, it is critical that supervisees know how to utilize and refer clients to services that offer 24-hour accessibility for crisis support as this can help improve therapeutic outcomes. Indeed, the number of individuals who seek out assistance in an immediate manner has increased due to the mobilization of 24-hour crisis intervention organizations (Roberts, 1991). Crisis counselors offer direct care and supervisees can improve their ability to offer such services by contacting their supervisors, but some form of resolution is still necessary upon departure from the crisis scene (Hipple & Beamish, 2007). This is where referrals to crisis hotlines, support groups, etc., become significant. Therefore, a supervisor and a supervisee can work together to make sure a crisis support plan is in place before a serious event occurs.

Here are a few scenarios related to critical incidents on the next page:

Medical Safety "Call 911."

Gilbert, a Licensed Clinical Social Worker, calls you to state a medical emergency occurred in his session with Ronnie, who has seizures in response to stress. Gilbert shares he had to call 911 when Ronnie began to seize in session. Gilbert reports Ronnie received medical attention, however Gilbert, in response to the event, is feeling guilt and worry about continuing with their trauma therapy.

Q: What role from The Empowerment Model would you start with to support your supervisee?
Q: What questions would you ask about Gilbert's experience to best support him?
Q: What safety measures need to be in place to support both Ronnie and Gilbert?

Physical Safety "It was a wild party."

Amanda, a new grad therapist, calls you to share that she arrived at her clients' mom Mindy and teenage daughter Ella's apartment for in-home therapy where daughter Ella recounted Mindy's relapse and partying behavior after sending Ella to a relative's over the weekend. Amanda reports she is struggling with the next steps due to

Mindy's relapse and worries for Ella's well-being in future situations.

Q: What role from The Empowerment Model would you start with to support your supervisee?

Q: How would you support Amanda in evaluating safety and reporting needs?

Q: What safety measures need to be in place to support both Mindy and Ella?

Critical Incidents "It was only for a second."

Helena, a Master's Level Counselor is reviewing her case file, when you observe a notation about Helena providing psychoeducation on drug exposure and children, referencing the week prior. When exploring the discrepancy with Helena in supervision, Helena reports that the baby put a pipe in its mouth for two seconds, the parent intervened, and Helena, upon determining the baby to be fine, continued with the session as usual. Helena is reporting to you that she wasn't concerned with drug exposure for the baby and thus did not seek supervision at the time of the incident.

Q: What role from The Empowerment Model would you start with to support your supervisee?
Q: Does this event represent a reportable critical incident? Why or why not?
Q: What steps are necessary to support Helena in her role?
Q: How would you encourage appropriate reporting of a critical incident for future reference?

Suicide Assessment "He said he was fine."

Edie, a recent graduate counselor, is staffing her case with you regarding Rich, a 56-year-old client who is retiring from his job of twenty years. She is sharing that he seems to be really struggling with the transition and made a statement in their last appointment which made her feel nervous and worried. As you engage Edie, you discover the client made some suicidal statements and Edie did not complete a suicide assessment to explore this further.

Q: What role from The Empowerment Model would you start with to support your supervisee?
Q. How can Edie support her client with any suicidal thoughts or actions?
Q: What documentation is needed to record and assess her client's current state?

Q. How can you support Edie in exploring her own reactions and biases about suicide to best support her client?

Conversely, a violation of the crisis support boundary would involve a supervisee becoming ill, for example, and calling a supervisor to request assistance with filling a prescription or to discuss a personal crisis (e.g., a sibling getting fired from a job). It should also be explained to a supervisee that if he or she experiences a personal crisis (e.g., depression, anxiety) that poses a risk to his or her emotional well-being and client services that although the supervisor will address the issue, the supervisee will subsequently be referred for psychotherapy. The point to emphasize is that supervisees will receive work-related crisis support from a supervisor as long as it stays within professional boundaries. Counseling is distinct from crisis intervention and clinical supervision ensures that critical decision-making skills will be acquired along with strategies for overcoming numerous obstacles to help stabilize a client who is experiencing a crisis.

Supporting Self-Care

The helping professional field is one that is immersed in challenges. Clients may relapse or be resistant to intervention, they may engage in threatening or dangerous behaviors, there are administrative requirements that must be met, and many other issues may arise. For supervisors in particular, being responsible for the services that supervisees provide and having to occasionally provide negative feedback can be stressful. Challenges that are specific to supervisees include being evaluated, having clinical work scrutinized on a regular basis, and meeting clients in the absence of a supervisor. All helping professionals have to deal with the personal difficulties they may face (e.g., health, relationships, financial difficulties, etc.) as emotional distress can directly influence professional competence if it is not addressed (Barnett & Molzon, 2014).

Supervisors who promote their psychological well-being by practicing good self-care help ensure their ongoing professionalism and model optimal ethical conduct for their supervisees. Similarly, supervisees should be encouraged to proactively practice self-care. Accordingly, both supervisors and supervisees should set healthy self-care boundaries. Self-care activities involve leaving unfinished work until the next day, saying no to tasks that are overwhelming, and taking a lunch break in which no work-related phone calls, documentation, etc., occur during the break (Norcross & Guy, 2007). The following examples of healthy boundaries accommodate these types of activities:

- Setting aside strict times for a lunch break
- Clearly defining work hours (e.g., 8 am to 4 pm or 9 am to 5 pm)
- Listing specific situations in which after-hour calls would be appropriate
- Setting limits for the number of clients a supervisee will work with during the week
- Discussing and/or setting limits for a comfortable workload (e.g., working with no more than 3 supervisees per month)

However, it is also important to maintain ethical boundaries in relation to self-care. For instance, spending personal time with a supervisee as a means of self-care is a violation of professional boundaries. This includes having dinner with a supervisee as it may create familiarity that may cause roles to become crossed (e.g., supervisor taking on a counselor role). The same scenarios pertain to supervisees and their clients. Overall, self-care boundaries should be fostered and reinforced in clinical supervision as this sustains emotionally healthy clinicians.

Documentation Needs

Supervisors oversee numerous aspects of clinical training, including documentation. According to *The ACA Code of Ethics*, counselors safeguard and maintain documentation that is necessary for professional services. Furthermore, proper record keeping and documentation protects counselors from allegations of professional negligence and ethical misconduct, maintains client confidentiality, and promotes the delivery of high-quality counseling services (Reamer, 2005). This means that in addition to encouraging optimal clinical practices, documentation is also necessary for litigious purposes. Supervisors can be held liable for violations made by a supervisee, especially if there is evidence of insufficient supervision in terms of record keeping. Thusly, supervisors should monitor supervisees' documentation practices and keep a record of counseling sessions and supervision meetings which involved a discussion of ethical or legal issues.

Another essential aspect of documentation involves safety planning, which entails making supervisees aware of the various types of safety issues that may arise during counseling. They should also be provided with training regarding how conflicts, harassment, or threats can be addressed, how to protect property, and how to deal with an assault if such an event occurs as well as the emotional aftermath of this type of trauma. Developing a written plan for safety during counseling sessions and while in the community helps prepare supervisees for unforeseeable events. The plan should include a list of possible crises and response strategies as well as contact information for members of a support team. This reduces the chances of serious emotional and/or physical harm, and ensures that a supervisee knows who to contact for timely support. An example of a standard safety plan can be found in Appendix B. Challenging and distressing situations are unavoidable in the counseling field, but the key to responding to crises appropriately and in a non-violent manner is being prepared for the unexpected. It must also be emphasized that a critical incident report needs to be made for any safety issue that arises.

Critical incident documentation refers to reporting an alleged or actual situation that poses a significant risk of substantial harm to the mental or physical health of a client or person associated with a client. Documenting a serious, threatening event reduces misunderstandings and the probability that important details will be forgotten. This emphasizes the importance of documenting such incidents soon after they occurred. Incident reporting becomes especially problematic if it is discovered that a supervisee is withholding information from a supervisor. Professional development requires proper disclosure, but policy also states that critical incidents must be documented.

Thorough documentation protects the welfare of the client, the supervisor and the supervisee, as well as the organization from liability and litigation. If a supervisor establishes a strict documentation procedure with the supervisee, this creates a platform in which both parties can regularly review reports to track a client's progress, the professional development of the supervisee, and the integrity of a supervisee's reporting habits. Regularly reviewing documents and openly discussing distressing counseling sessions is also an important risk management approach. These strategies augment good faith efforts to provide optimal clinical supervision. It also encourages supervisees to avoid documentation violations such as failing to report critical incidents.

Legal Safety "He's not allowed to be here."

Ricardo, a Marriage and Family Therapist Candidate, calls to share the events of his session with Amelia, who is engaging in individual therapy. Amelia reports that as she was entering the building for her appointment, her ex-fiancée drove past, with whom she has a restraining order for former domestic violence. Amelia processed her fears with Ricardo, who felt obligated to escort Amelia to her car after the appointment in an effort to promote her safety.

Q: What role from The Empowerment Model would you start with to support your supervisee?
Q: What questions would you explore with Ricardo regarding the situation and safety?
Q: What safety measures need to be in place to support his client Amelia?

Confidentiality Needs "It just slipped."

Becky, a seasoned, Licensed Professional Counselor, comes to you as a colleague for consultation as she feels she broke confidentiality. Becky describes how she was in a meeting with a caseworker who was on an old case they had worked together, and Becky had updated the caseworker on the family that she still sees.

Q: What role from The Empowerment Model would you start with to support your supervisee?
Q. As a consultation colleague, what do you recommend?
Q. If this was a newer counselor, would your recommendation(s) change?

Release of Information *(ROI) "I needed to clarify."*

Yolanda, a Marriage and Family Therapist Candidate, working with a family for the past 6 months, is a new graduate and came to supervision with a concern about an ROI. Yolanda discloses to you that she forgot to get an ROI signed to talk to a grandmother who lives in the home with the family. When calling to set the next appointment, the grandmother answered the phone and asked how counseling was going, as the grandmother felt that the family was still not doing well. Out of an urge to justify her work, Yolanda talked at length about the family, including barriers to sessions and family progress.

Q: What role from The Empowerment Model would you start with to support your supervisee?

Q. How do you explore the ROI mistake and implications for confidentiality?

Q: How do you support Yolanda with accountability and confidentiality in working with the family?

Documentation "I'm way behind."

Ginny, a Marriage and Family Therapist Candidate, smiles sheepishly in your office when asked about the progress of her notes and file compliance. Ginny reports she is struggling to compile the notes while attending to clients, case management, and her own family.

Q: What role from The Empowerment Model would you start with to support your supervisee?

Q: How would you explore Ginny's time management skills?

Q: What support can you offer with deadlines in place to achieve paperwork compliance?

Professionalism "The neighborhood was whack."

Ebonee is a new counselor enjoying her work with at-risk teens in urban areas. Ebonee has submitted her progress report for proofing prior to sharing them with the assigned treatment team. When reviewing her notes about her client's living situation, you read language that depicts some negative emotions about her client's housing including neighbors and overall cleanliness of the location.

Q: What role from The Empowerment Model would you start with to support your supervisee?
Q: How would you go about exploring Ebonee's reaction and inclination to include choice words regarding her client's living situation?
Q: How would you engage Ebonee in her professional development including cultural competency?

Approach to Clinical Supervision in the Community System

What is a Community Program?

A community program is one which offers counseling services for personal issues such as anxiety disorder, depression, career or academic issues, family or relationship problems, behavioral difficulties, etc., to clients from various populations (Haynes et al., 2003). In contrast to individual therapy where a counselor works closely with a client in a private practice to promote therapeutic progress through rapport and strategies such as guided discovery, some community programs have on-site counselors who are available to provide services when a client visits a site for immediate counseling. Furthermore, community programs may also be an alternative to medical counseling for individuals suffering from substance abuse disorder or other issues that necessitate intensive therapeutic services. Some people may even be court-mandated to enroll in such programs.

Community counseling is typically located in close proximity to where clients live, which makes it more accessible for people with limited transportation or those who want to avoid seeking treatment through a medical facility. In addition, community counseling services tend to be specialized; therefore, the helping professionals in these programs often have a specific skill set. They may work from the program location on different days of the week and also provide private counseling in between. Community programs allow helping professionals with specialized skills to target issues where they are occurring in order to stop the progression of a serious issue before it becomes a problematic disorder or disease that is harder to address, diagnose, and effectively treat. Accordingly, a clinical supervisor who works in a community program is generally assigned to more than one counseling trainee. There is also the possibility that trainees may be supervised by several clinical counselors in a community organization (Haynes et al., 2003). For instance, there may be a site supervisor, an administrative supervisor, and a group supervisor who oversees group sessions for supervisees.

Community Coordination

Similar to the supervisory relationship that is established for counselors in private practices, community coordination facilitates the rendering of services through community programs. However, collaboration within a community setting is not just between a supervisor and supervisee; it extends to additional professionals who work for the program such as a program director, social worker, probation officer, etc. In other words, professional teams work together in community programs. Indeed, through the collaborative effort of each of the professionals, which includes a clinical supervisor and supervisee under training, the team should be able to identify environmental factors that hinder a client's development (Lewis et al., 2002). In particular, the supervisee who works with clients as well as the clinical supervisor who oversees the sessions, use comprehensive listening skills to understand clients' goals as well as that of the program. Problems that are observed during sessions can be discussed with the professional team (with a release on file for all parties) who can alert other community groups about common concerns related to health issues (e.g., mental health, alcoholism, etc.). The team can subsequently establish alliances with additional organizations that are working toward making positive changes in the community. A team meeting in which the strengths and resources of each member is evaluated helps facilitate systemic change (Lewis et al., 2002).

In reference to clinical supervision, it is especially essential to identify skills that the counselor (supervisee) brings into the collaboration as the counselor is one of the main individuals who have the opportunity to influence client outcomes through his or her close interactions with the community. The counselor also has the potential to emphasize the urgency for change through proper documentation and the interpretation of critical observations. Collaboration with the professional team can also be expanded to stakeholders who have the means to propagate changes within a community program that will benefit clients (Lewis et al., 2002). That is, while working with clients, a counselor may discover systemic factors or recurring themes that have become barriers to growth and development. Counselors are quite often one of the first helping professionals to notice specific difficulties in the environment that are negatively affecting clients. This may elicit a desire to initiate a change in the environment or community program that would prevent some of the problems people face every day.

Irrespective of the target that needs to change, the process that leads to a change encompasses leadership, persistence, vision, collaboration, systems analysis, and persuasive data. The counselor (supervisee) is often the right individual to take on this type of initiative. Therefore, counselors can advocate for clients in private as well as community settings. They can also be especially helpful to community programs by offering specific skills such as interpersonal relations, training, communication, and research-based data.

The following vignette presents a communication-related scenario that may occur in a community setting:

> **Written/Email Correspondence "Reply all."**
>
> George, a therapist intern, is printing case notes for his file for review and asks if emails should be included. Upon agreement, George begins printing emails when you notice names of third parties in a "reply all" fashion. When asked, George reports he doesn't know their role in the

case and had responded to the caseworker
accordingly to schedule a team meeting.

Q: What role from The Empowerment Model
would you start with to support your
supervisee?
Q: How do you explore releases with George?
Q: What steps should be taken to secure
confidential information?

Documentation and Mandatory Reporting

For every health profession, clinical documentation is
required as stated by ethics codes, regulations and laws,
institutional policies, and practice guidelines (e.g., ACA
Code of Ethics). Thorough, efficient, and timely
documentation of services that are rendered by counselors
serve several purposes, including the following (Falender
& Shafranske, 2004):

- It helps a busy counselor remember specific details
  about a client's therapy from session to session,
  thereby enhancing the provision of high quality
  counseling services.
- It provides members of a professional team with
  information which enables each of them to better

understand how to coordinate care based on each other's therapeutic efforts and the observed results.

- It facilitates continuity of care if a client ends counseling but decides to return at a later time for services with the same counselor or another professional.

- It is a strategy for risk management as the documentation is a tangible record of all rendered services, consultation with supervisors or colleagues, the counselor's decision-making process, the counselor's role in the therapeutic intervention, and the observed outcomes.

Even though supervisors are familiar with and adhere to the documentation requirements for clinical services (e.g., assessment, intervention, phone calls between sessions or during crises, etc.), there may be some who do not fully recognize the significance and value of both the supervisor and the supervisee creating reports of each supervisory meeting. A written record of these sessions can (1) increase a supervisee's accountability, (2) reduce potential misunderstandings, (3) be an excellent resource for both parties to review in order to track a supervisee's progress as well as the personal development of clients, and (4) it is an essential risk management tool that serves as a tangible report of the events that transpired during supervision, as well as evidence of a supervisor's good faith efforts to offer high quality clinical supervision (Falender & Shafranske, 2004).

> ### *Mandatory Reporting "It will ruin my rapport."*
>
> Craig is the individual counselor for the mother on an open DHS case. He has been providing sessions weekly for about 6 months. During supervision, he tells you that at the last session, 5 days ago, his client disclosed that she would spank the children and sometimes she would leave bruises on their buttocks and legs. Mom currently does not have the children in her custody and all of her visits are supervised.
>
> Q: What role from The Empowerment Model would you start with to support your supervisee?
> Q. There are concerns that require Craig's attention, what are they?
> Q. How would you guide Craig to resolve these concerns?

CONTINUED: Reporting to the Abuse Hotline "But it's not happening now."

Q: What role from The Empowerment Model would you start with to support your supervisee?

Q. Using the example above, how would the required report be made?

Q: How do you explore Craig's understanding of mandatory reporting and confidentiality?

Q: What information would be obtained and what would Craig share with the abuse hotline?

County of Incident Reporting "He won't engage after this."

Bill, a Licensed Social Worker, comes to supervision as the individual therapist for Simon, a 14-year-old boy. In session, Simon discloses that he tried cocaine over the past weekend for the first time. Bill thinks he does not have to disclose this to the county, despite state social services having custody, this only occurring one time, and the client reporting "not liking it". Bill also states concern that if he discloses this information, Simon will end sessions with him and will not engage in counseling services elsewhere.

Q: What role from The Empowerment Model would you start with to support your supervisee?

Q. Is this incident reportable?

Q: How can you support Bill in addressing current safety concerns with his client, including an understanding of state involvement?

Q: Would your recommendations be different if this client was not in the custody of the state?

Although documentation is a requirement for all helping professions, administrators of community programs are becoming increasingly accountable for the quality of care that clients receive as well as the cost-efficiency of rendered services (Smith et al., 1997). Quality of care is often a difficult aspect of counseling to monitor, especially when the intervention involves managing a chronic disorder. In community settings, a team-based quality review appears to positively influence the quality of documentation. During a scheduled meeting, the team can address whether a supervisee's documents comprehensively cover areas such as intake, assessment, diagnosis, intervention planning, and the provision of clinical services. Additional areas to review are the supervisee's reports regarding therapeutic management and client progress as well as whether the documents reflect regulatory or contractual requirements (e.g., are the procedure codes correct).

Over the years, focus has increasingly shifted toward efficiency and outcome measures, making the quality and accuracy of clinical documentation even more important (Baker, Shanfield, & Schnee, 2000). In addition, stakeholders of community programs often request clinical reports to obtain data that is required for evaluating client outcomes. However, accurate documentation is critical for community programs because additional professionals may need to periodically view a client's report in order to make well-informed decisions. For instance, there may be situations in which additional or more intensive intervention becomes necessary and proper documentation on the counselor's part may provide strong support for the provision of extended services. This is especially the case for individuals who have been court-mandated to receive services through a community program as social workers, probation officers, and even judges may request a client's clinical counseling records. In such cases, not only is documentation required, it may also be mandatory.

There are certain situations that a counselor must report and it is important to make clients aware of the limitations to confidentiality. The law requires a helping professional to report incidents where a client has become a danger to him- or herself or to others as well as cases of child/adolescent neglect or abuse (SAMHSA, 2000). However, counselors typically need specific information before they can file the required reports. For instance, if a client says, "I often have thoughts of harming myself," this issue does not need to be reported to anyone other than the supervisor, although it still needs to be addressed through counseling, an active suicide assessment, and monitoring. Conversely, if the client says statements such as, "I just want to die or I'm going to commit suicide," assessment should occur immediately with the supervisor and the authorities may need to be contacted to quickly address the needs of the client. Similarly, if a client in court-mandated substance treatment says, "I'm meeting someone tomorrow to buy drugs," a report would need to be filed with a social worker, probation officer, or other designated authority member. With mandated clients, counselors need to explain the type of information that will be reported, who it will be reported to, and have the client sign an informed consent form or document outlining the limits of confidentiality before counseling begins (ACA, 2014).

Helping professionals who are mandated reporters (e.g., supervisees) must be given documentation that clearly outlines the reporting requirements. For instance, child abuse, elderly abuse, and safety concerns such as observed substance abuse are incidents that necessitate the mandated reporter designation. In addition, helping professionals should understand that they are protected from liability for good faith reports which may later be deemed as erroneous or unsubstantiated. Similarly, programs that provide mandated services should establish a protocol for handling legal reporting requirements. This may entail having a protocol in place which dictates that a counselor must discuss any disconcerting cases with a supervisor to determine if an incident is reportable. If it is, the supervisor may discuss the issue with a clinical director and if additional information is requested through a subpoena, for example, the director could seek legal representation by contacting a lawyer.

It is also essential to orient new counselors (supervisees) to the program's reporting guidelines, procedures, and policies. The policies should include provisions that require counselors to inform their supervisors or appropriate program staff members of a report that has been made. In addition, the policies must emphasize the importance of consulting with a supervisor as soon as a concern regarding the need to report an incident arises. We have included examples of mandatory reporting and critical incident forms for clinical supervision in Appendix

B as well as examples of a suicide risk assessment and individual/family safety plans for counseling in Appendix C. Most community programs have a designated staff member in place who can develop and keep record of an incident report form that ensures relevant information is obtained, as well as handle additional legal matters related to mandatory reporting. This individual may also be designated to help counselors prepare for a testimony in court if a particular case necessitates it.

Preparation for Court Testimony

According to *The ACA Code of Ethics*, section *B.2.d Court-Ordered Disclosure*, (ACA, 2014):

> When ordered by a court to release confidential or privileged information without a client's permission, counselors seek to obtain written, informed consent from the client or take steps to prohibit the disclosure or have it limited as narrowly as possible because of potential harm to the client or counseling relationship.

An aspect of clinical supervision that is often neglected unless a supervisee is faced with such a challenge during training, is being prepared to testify in a courtroom. Counselors are increasingly being subpoenaed for courtroom testimonies, especially for cases that involve child custody arrangements (Colby & Long, 1994). Unfortunately, counselors are often ill-prepared to adequately represent the helping professional field in court or be proficient witnesses for clients. Furthermore, insufficient knowledge about how the legal system operates and specific courtroom procedures can increase the probability that counselors will make ethical violations. More specifically, being inadequately prepared by supervisors and attorneys can be a distressing and even traumatizing experience for a counselor, especially a new supervisee. This is because the counselor may not be able to effectively address difficult questions when he or she is on the witness stand or handle the arduous cross-examination. A lack of preparation could ultimately damage a client's court case and lead to a misrepresentation of the helping profession (Colby & Long, 1994). With this in mind, we've included an example of questions a supervisor and supervisee might use to prepare for court testimony in Appendix B.

Supervisors are tasked with having a sound understanding of the legal issues involved in their profession as well as any changes that occur in their specific field. In *The ACA Code of Ethics, standard F.7.a* states that, "Counselor educators who are responsible for developing, implementing, and supervising educational programs are skilled as teachers and practitioners. They are knowledgeable regarding the ethical, legal, and regulatory aspects of the profession; are skilled in applying that knowledge; and make students and supervisees aware of their responsibilities (ACA, 2014)." In reference to clinical supervision, this standard indicates that because counselors are more frequently being subpoenaed to appear in court and testify on their clients' behalf, they should be well-prepared beforehand. Accordingly, clinical supervisors are obligated to train supervisees about their legal and ethical duties when they are summoned to provide a testimony in a courtroom.

In addition to distributing learning material regarding courtroom procedures and additional aspects of the law that pertain to being a witness for clients, they also need to acquire relevant knowledge about legal topics. It is also beneficial for supervisors and their supervisees to consult with helping professionals who previously served as key witnesses in their clients' court cases. Gaining experience from other counselors who have provided court testimonies on several different cases emphasizes the significance of making sure counselors are prepared to testify in the courtroom because they may be subpoenaed at any time throughout their careers. Therefore, both time and extra effort need to be channeled into establishing curricula that enhance learning as well as skills that are needed to effectively provide a professional, prepared testimony. Supervisees who are thoroughly prepared and well-educated in these matters have a heightened ability to represent clients, the helping profession, and themselves.

In response to this need, *four categories of counselor education* have been established (Colby & Long, 1994): preparation before court, a supervisee's role in the courtroom, techniques for answering tough questions, and courtroom etiquette. The following scenario involves staying in the therapeutic role when faced with an ethical dilemma:

Staying in the Therapeutic Role "I don't like him."

Steve, a Masters-level Counselor comes to supervision to staff a case where he is providing individual counseling to Stacy, a 13-year-old girl. Steve reports his client has talked at length in session about how much she does not like her father. Stacy currently lives with her mom. In session, Stacy describes times in which her father was "mean." Her descriptions are of concern, but none of the content she has shared is reportable to the child abuse hotline. Steve is feeling very angry toward the father and just recently received a letter from the mom's attorney, requesting recommendations for court to determine if supervised visits should happen between Stacy and her father. Steve wants to say "No," the father should not get visits based on what the client has shared about past interactions with him, and wants to recommend that no visits should occur.

Q: What role from The Empowerment Model would you start with to support your supervisee?

Q. How can Steve stay in his role as the individual counselor and still advocate for the needs of his client, Stacy?

Q. If Steve makes the recommendation he feels is appropriate, what are the risks to him, to you as his supervisor, the client and the relationship with her father?

One of the most important ways to prepare for court is to review the quality and accuracy of previous documentation. As documentation is a requirement for all helping professionals, it should not be too difficult to obtain the necessary reports for the courtroom. Lawyers may ask for a variety of information from the records, therefore, counselors should have a copy of a client's complete record even if the lawyer only requests to see specific records related to the nature of the court case. In addition, if a client's records are subpoenaed, it is important to document this in the client's file and immediately contact the individual to make him or her aware of the breach of confidentiality (Colby & Long, 1994). The client may want to speak in person or over the phone to gain a better understanding of what is happening and to possibly discuss apprehensions. This meeting should be documented as well.

Another key preparation strategy is meeting with the lawyer in order to determine exactly which documents will need to be presented and the questions that will be potentially asked in the courtroom. The lawyer may even conduct a mock cross-examination to help prepare the counselor for what may happen in court. Additional details that can be discussed in this meeting include courtroom etiquette, which refers to both dressing and behaving in a professional manner as well as demonstrating confident body language (Colby & Long, 1994). In general, the same demeanor that is exhibited during counseling sessions should be displayed in the courtroom. Furthermore, lawyers who perform the cross examination may try to discredit a witness through rapid questioning, badgering, or intimidation, but practicing ways to stay calm can help counselors overcome such problems. Overall, the supervisor, supervisee, and lawyer who are representing a client must work together to ensure that the counselor is well-prepared to present the appropriate records, answer difficult questions, and be cross-examined. The first time a counselor testifies on behalf of a client will be a stressful situation, but as with other counseling services, the ability to provide strong testimony will improve over time and with practice.

Clinical Boundaries with Professionals

Confidentiality

Clinical supervision meetings, counseling sessions, and any documentation that is associated with counseling are confidential according to *The ACA Code of Ethics*. However, counselors are also required by the Ethics Code to discuss the limitations of confidentiality, which include the release of information for clients who were mandated to receive counseling and the duty to warn in cases of potential emotional and/or physical harm. This means that confidentiality is limited in situations that present a serious concern in regard to the professional or ethical conduct of a supervisee or a client's safety. Accordingly, it is the responsibility of clinical supervisors to ensure that there is appropriate documentation of such situations and that the records are stored and kept confidential. The limitations to confidentiality and possible situations in which confidentiality would need to be breached should be discussed with clients at the initiation of counseling.

Circumstances where confidentiality may be broken include intent to harm self or others, minor abuse or neglect, or drug and alcohol treatment. For example, when a school-aged client discloses in counseling that they want to harm a peer and identify a plan to do so, notifying school officials or engaging community supports can keep the identified peer safe under a duty to warn. The same guidelines would apply in regard to acts of domestic violence (e.g., client reveals the intent to engage in such acts) as the client poses a serious risk to others. In general, when the limitation of confidentiality or the duty to warn are being explored, the four following factors should be considered:

- Does a professional relationship exist that would dictate disclosure?
- Has a serious threat been identified?
- Has the client named or described a specific victim?
- Does the client pose a serious, foreseeable risk to others?

The presence of one or more of these elements would provide sound ethical and legal justification for the disclosure of confidential information.

Here is an example of such an incident:

Safety Concern "It's just a date."

Rebecca, a Licensed Professional Counselor, is working with 16-year-old Kate as her individual therapist. Kate is disclosing that she will be sneaking out of the foster home later that night to go on a date with a boy she met online and knows Rebecca can't share it because it's confidential. Rebecca agrees that confidentiality is important, however, she has safety concerns for Kate in meeting up with a stranger at an undisclosed location.

Q: What role from The Empowerment Model would you start with to support your supervisee?
Q: What steps should be taken to address the safety concerns identified?
Q: How would you support Rebecca in disclosing decisions around safety and confidentiality with Kate to best support their ongoing therapeutic relationship?

There is an additional aspect of confidentiality within clinical supervision in that before counseling services can be provided, supervisees must disclose their status as trainees. In addition, supervisees have to make the potential clients aware of how the supervision training affects the limitations of confidentiality and provide them with written disclosure information including contact information for the supervisor should the client have any concerns. The disclosure should include a specific description of who will be able to access the client's record as well as how the documents will be stored, reviewed, or transmitted if it becomes necessary. The disclosure statement should also explain that supervisors discuss the rights of clients with supervisees, including the protection of client confidentiality and privacy in the supervisory relationship. Supervisors should also ensure clients of the confidentiality of the services rendered and the qualifications of the supervisees who are rendering the services. Informing clients at the initiation of counseling allows them to decide whether they want to continue receiving services and prevents potential legal issues from developing. If a client decides to proceed with counseling, a supervisee must obtain client permission before using any information pertaining to counseling sessions for training purposes (ACA, 2014).

Texting Multiple Parties "What did I miss?"

Serephina is the foster parent to client Ernesto, who is a minor working with Eleanor, a Marriage and Family Therapist. Serephina sends a text to Eleanor and Ernesto's biological father Pedro, sharing escalation of Ernesto's negative behaviors after sessions with dad and asking for Eleanor to disclose what is happening during the sessions to make him so upset.

Q: What role from The Empowerment Model would you start with to support your supervisee?
Q: How should Eleanor respond to address the concerns of the foster parent?
Q: What boundaries can be in place for future communication between Eleanor and the foster parent?

Community Collaboration

Working closely with other helping professionals means that an extra effort must be made to develop collaboration and mutual trust (Haynes et al., 2003). Collaboration is defined as the joining together of two parties through purposeful conversation and an environment of trust. In addition, each person values and recognizes the significance of the relationship. Accordingly, mutually desired goals are established through problem-solving. In relation to clinical supervision, collaboration is a partnership in which a supervisor honors a supervisee's perspectives and expertise, while creating an environment that is conducive to change rather than coercive. Previous reports indicate that harmful boundaries to collaboration include the power differential of the supervisory relationship, its evaluative components, and anxiety that usually develops as this tends to overshadow the potential for professional growth (Bean, Davis, & Davey, 2014). These factors are counter-intuitive to the goals of clinical supervision.

Conversely, a collaborative effort creates a supportive context that promotes relaxed alertness, a heightened learning experience, and autonomy. Collaboration also influences additional aspects of clinical supervision such as available resources, the training setting, and a supervisee's progression through different developmental stages. Supervision should be viewed as a learning partnership and when this occurs it can reduce unwarranted stress, facilitate transparency in learning, encourage an open mind in relation to feedback, and empower the supervisee (Burg et al, 2017; Friedlander & Shaffer, 2014). Empowerment positively impacts counselors' work ethic and the welfare of clients.

At the beginning of supervision, the collaborative framework and intention as well as boundaries and limitations should be explained to the supervisee. Body language and verbiage influence collaborative efforts as well. Statements that help facilitate collaboration include, "your opinions are important; feel free to ask questions at any time; and we are both learning and growing so this is a good place to share wisdom with one another." Similarly, an important boundary that should be discussed early on is that a supervisee should not struggle with a counseling issue for a substantial amount of time before revealing it to a supervisor.

An additional boundary includes, for example, remaining professional when providing feedback to a supervisee by refraining from using personal analogies outside the realm of counseling as a form of encouragement and avoiding physical contact if negative feedback must be given. Supervisees must also be provided with boundaries in regard to personal issues they may want to discuss as only that which promotes professional growth is appropriate within the supervisory setting. It is also important that they understand that a collaborative partnership does not mean they can always speak their mind freely, especially if the feelings they intend to express have negative connotations towards a supervisor's feedback. Reflective conversations are an essential component of collaboration that supports learning, but both parties must also remain respectful at all times (Gray & Smith, 2009). Overall, a supervisor's capacity to be attuned to a supervisee's strengths and needs as well as clear communication from both parties facilitates a harmonious balance between guiding a supervisee toward autonomy and challenging him or her when it is deemed appropriate. This type of collaboration leads to self-sufficiency.

Dual Roles

There are situations in which supervisors may inadvertently enter dual roles such as counseling their supervisees or working with community program personnel who ask a supervisor to hold too many roles. In addition, there are instances where a supervisor may even become a substance abuse sponsor in a community program for a former supervisee (SAMHSA, 2009). This reflects a dual relationship in clinical supervision as the supervisor initially played a professional role, but at another time point engaged in a different relationship with a supervisee that transcended a professional supervisory relationship. The degree of potential harm or actual harm that may occur as a result of dual roles generally varies, and some of the negative outcomes of dual roles may not become apparent until later on. The issue that makes this type of dual role especially problematic is the potential abuse of power, the probability that the change in the relationship will impair the supervisee's judgment, and the risk of exploitation (SAMHSA, 2009).

In regard to avoiding instances where a supervisee is unexpectedly counseled, it is important for a supervisor to remember that facilitating counselor development and ensuring optimal client care entails steering away from discussions that encroach upon personal issues. That is, the primary goal of supervision is to assist supervisees in becoming better counselors, not trying to help them resolve their personal problems. Having a thorough understanding of the difference between providing clinical supervision and counseling helps supervisors remain objective. For instance, the purpose of clinical supervision is to improve client care and job performance, while the purpose of counseling is to foster personal growth, positive behavioral changes, and better self-understanding (SAMHSA, 2009). Similarly, the basic process that underlies clinical supervision entails teaching or further enhancing specific skills and evaluating a supervisee's job performance, while the counseling process may involve cognitive, behavioral, or affective approaches (e.g., exploration, listening, coaching). Focusing on these types of differences helps a supervisor avoid engaging in dual roles such as counseling a supervisee. Furthermore, if a supervisee's personal issues begin to arise during supervision, the key questions a supervisor should answer include:

- Do the supervisee's personal issues affect his or her delivery of quality care?
- What impact will the issues have on the client?
- What resources are being used to resolve the issue outside of the counseling dyad?

Answering these questions helps a supervisor determine when a supervisee needs to be referred to a different professional who can provide counseling, and in doing so prevents problems that may occur due to dual roles. Most importantly, a supervisor must make sure that a supervisee understands that outside therapy or counseling is a necessity when personal matters interfere with quality care (SAMHSA, 2009). It is the responsibility of the supervisor to identify issues that may be impairing a supervisee's performance and make any referrals that are necessary, but counseling the supervisee is not one of the supervisor's roles.

A specific issue that often arises in community settings involves a supervisor having to take on several roles that fall under both clinical supervision and administrative supervision. More specifically, a supervisor who works in a community program may be asked to oversee both supervision and managerial aspects of the organization (SAMHSA, 2009). This may entail structuring staff work; evaluating personnel for compensation and promotions; performing planning tasks; defining the requirements of clinical competence; coordinating, delegating, and organizing work; interviewing, selecting, hiring, and firing personnel; and managing the community program. In addition to these administrative duties, clinical supervisors may also be responsible for conducting quality assurance reviews, facilitating improvement aspects of the organization, they may have their own case-load, and they may have several supervisees to train. In such cases, it is essential that a supervisor remains aware of what role he or she is playing as well as how to exercise the authority that has been given by administration.

Having to execute numerous roles can hinder a supervisor's ability to carry out individual roles properly. Therefore, it is critical that a supervisor is cautious in terms of acknowledging difficulties that are faced before any problems can begin to affect performance, an evaluation, or even possible compensation increases

(SAMHSA, 2009). Delegating certain administrative functions that do not have to be performed by a supervisor to financial services, human resources, or the legal department, for example, can help address this type of issue. At times it may also be useful to ask for input from other professionals about whether objectivity and competence is consistently being exemplified when numerous roles are being executed. Organizations do not always have the resources to hire several professionals for different positions and this means that supervisors will often be faced with dual roles. Taking active steps to properly balance each of the roles prevents work-place burnout and impaired performance.

Advocating for Client Needs

The *ACA Code of Ethics* explains that counselors are advocates for clients facing obstacles or barriers that hinder their growth and development (ACA, 2014). Furthermore, advocacy encompasses the use of empowerment strategies and direct counseling to help clients bring their lives into perspective. Supervisees who become competent at this level will be able to identify cultural, social, economic, and political factors as well as strengths and resources that affect a client (Lewis et al., 2002; Ratts & Hutchins, 2009). They will also be able to recognize signs that indicate that a client's concerns or behavior reflect responses to internalized oppression. In addition, they can train clients in self-advocacy skills as well as in the development and execution of self-advocacy action plans. Advocacy efforts on the part of supervisees also entails negotiating relevant services for clients, identifying potential allies who can provide additional support, and carrying out a plan of action on behalf of a client. Nevertheless, client consent must be obtained before a supervisee can initiate advocacy efforts that are geared toward finding a solution to barriers and obstacles that limit client access and thereby improve the provision of services that promote therapeutic progress.

Advocacy "I think it could help."

Albert, an unlicensed therapist, wants to advocate for his client Ari to receive contact with her family in engaging in steady substance treatment for the past three months. Albert attempted to reach the case worker for the past two weeks to share progress and recommend visitation.

Q: What role from The Empowerment Model would you start with to support your supervisee?

Q: What questions would you ask about Albert's recommendations and role with his client Ari?

Q: What steps are appropriate to take next in Ari's case?

It is important for helping professionals to remember that the purpose of client advocacy is to promote changes that will enhance quality of life and not to fulfill personal objectives on the part of the client or supervisee. For example, a counselor who brings to the attention of a supervisor or organization that a client should be allowed to decide if he or she can provide gifts (e.g., monetary or material) to a helping professional is not demonstrating advocacy competence. This type of conduct reflects personal interests and does not promote a better quality of life or an improved provision of services for the client. A supervisor can address this problem by exploring the underlying reason for presenting this type of issue. More specifically, this scenario depicts a change in the working relationship that may have inadvertently been misconstrued by the supervisee as an advocacy effort. To avoid such violations, it is important to describe in detail the purpose of client advocacy and situations in which it is appropriate. Establishing boundaries for advocacy efforts is essential as well. The key to demonstrating advocacy competence is being able to properly identify barriers to well-being or needed resources, and client advocacy is especially beneficial for clients who have (Haynes et al., 2003):

- Little experience in terms of exercising their rights
- Low socioeconomic status and may be uninformed about their rights
- Limited access to extended services (e.g., group therapy, psychiatric services)
- A mental disability that limits the understanding of their rights and services to which they are entitled

Helping professionals need to be able to function as competent advocates for their clients, especially those who are marginally acculturated and require remediation from an issue that developed due to oppression, discrimination, or negligence. Accordingly, it is the supervisor's duty to convey the significance of advocacy interventions.

Research Study Results and The Empowerment Model

In an effort to further explore the implications of The Empowerment Model of Clinical Supervision, a research study was completed from October 2018 to April 2019 within the Griffith Centers for Children, a community mental health agency serving at risk youth and families in the state of Colorado. Study participants included four (4) clinical supervisors and thirty-three (33) supervisees in offices located in Denver, Grand Junction, and Greeley, Colorado.

Study participants completed a consent form to engage in this study that outlined expectations, study purpose, and how the data would be used, as well as participation being voluntary. Supervisees ranged in age from 23 to 67 years of age and 29 out of 33 supervisees held a master's degree at time of employment at Griffith. Supervisees were randomly assigned to the control group (Group A) or the experimental group (Group B), taking into account their office location to allow for exploration of trends based on environmental differences. Group A participants were asked to complete a pre-test, post-test, and one supervision evaluation at the start of the study and one supervision evaluation at the end of the study. Each supervision evaluation included one evaluation completed by the supervisee and one evaluation completed by their supervisor that was an evaluation of their skills and competencies (see Appendix A). Group B participants were asked to complete a pre-test, post-test, and supervision evaluations monthly, resulting in data from the supervisee's evaluation on their own performance as well as the assigned supervisor's evaluation of their skills.

Supervisors were asked to engage with research investigators in order to introduce the model followed by meetings on a one-to-one basis weekly to monthly to explore their awareness of engaging supervisees within roles of teacher, researcher, leader, consultant, and colleague. Evaluations of supervisor consistency and engagement within each role were recorded for performance within this model. As the study began, one supervisor was omitted from the study due to seeking new employment, preventing data and participation in the Denver office for the purpose of this study, which included six identified participants. Several supervisees were also omitted from this study due to seeking new employment, resulting in 21 participants remaining from the 27 supervisees available for participation over the course of six months.

Of the 21 participants, 10 were assigned to Group A, and 11 were assigned to Group B. The analysis involved the Wilcoxon Rank Sum Test, a non-parametric test, due to our data reflecting non-linear points of growth based on self-reports and supervisor reports. The findings showed supervisee growth and improvement of their skills and clinical development over six months. Supervisor evaluations reflected more significant growth related to their supervisees' skills, most often reflecting elements within the category of The Clinical Counseling Process. Two participants showed a decline in skills indicated over the course of six months. It is hypothesized that this decline reflects organizational changes including a paperwork change and implementation after a formal audit as well as a decline in performance as these supervisees moved towards leaving the agency. Their exit was recorded shortly thereafter as part of their identified next steps in wrapping up goals within their supervisory relationship.

In contrast to the growth trends from participants themselves, when evaluating the supervisors' evaluations of their supervisees, significant improvement was found for elements within the categories of General Supervision, The Administrative Counseling Process, The Clinical Counseling Process, and The Conceptualization Process. There were no significant improvements that were identified in terms of Professional Communication, which could indicate the ongoing difficulty of navigating complex treatment teams and case management needs related to communication, or the limited communication needs of a standard outpatient model of therapeutic care.

One challenge that was not originally anticipated in our study involved the steady reports of supervisees ranking themselves with average scores over the course of the study, indicating that they believed their skills remained within mid-performance levels throughout the six months. This implies that there was no significant difference between Group A and Group B participants when evaluating the progression of supervision and the development of clinical skills per self-report. In exploring these results with the supervisors who engaged their supervisees monthly, we learned that the supervisors also saw trends of modest reporting from supervisees in skill development, most likely from a perspective place of continual improvement and some lack of predictability in client care that would prevent supervisee assumptions of mastery. Research findings also reflected individual self-reporting numbers between the designated scales of the Supervision Evaluation, which resulted in coding as the lower numeral (e.g., 2.5 became 2) which could account for some lack of significance recorded. In response to this user error, we would edit instructions on the Supervision Evaluation form to encourage commitment to the standardized numerical system that was utilized.

Supervisor performance for the duration of this study reflected frequent roles of the teacher evolving into the researcher and consultant. This was most reflected in the category of The Clinical Counseling Process as supervisees became more comfortable or confident in their skill sets, including engagement of clients in direct service work. Roles of the leader and colleague were found most frequently in supervisor modeling of communication within community contact or treatment team collaboration, of which supervisees were generally more likely to indicate average performance for themselves in these areas.

Supervisors who participated in this study also reflected on the process of implementing The Empowerment Model of Clinical Supervision with their team members, reporting that they had experience in leadership roles including current positions as supervisors at Griffith Centers for Children prior to the study. This could account for the personality characteristics and rapport recorded within the study, as supervisors had already established their roles and fostered collaboration with team members prior to the study. In other words, the difficulty or ease of adopting The Empowerment Model of Clinical Supervision could vary for supervisors recently promoted into this role or those who has joined a team in a leadership role for the first time.

Furthermore, research would require a larger sample size as well as the evaluation of counselor trends in underestimating skill set and potential growth in self-reports. Another consideration would involve implementing an in-depth training with supervisors prior to selecting this model for successful adoption into an agency or community mental health setting. Lastly, taking into consideration the training differences between the various disciplines of mental health providers (e.g., LPC, LCSW, LMFT) could warrant further discussion about the strengths of skill sets prior to the start of the supervisory relationship between a supervisor and supervisee.

Final Reflection of Supervision and The Empowerment Model

Clinical supervision is a disciplined working alliance between a supervisor and a supervisee. Supervisors are tasked with gaining knowledge that is necessary to exemplify professionalism and competence that supervisees will model. However, both parties should be open to learning from one another and examining counseling skills through reflection. There are a number of components that facilitate successful training which include documentation practices, establishing professional boundaries, various facets of community counseling, crisis support, and mandatory reporting. Accordingly, some trainees will demonstrate skilled and effective counseling, while others may make more mistakes than expected, but both aspects of supervision provide an opportunity to learn. In other words, additional knowledge can be gained from efficient clinical training, but mistakes also indicate the types of techniques or approaches that may need to be emphasized in the future. Overall, the significance of this multifaceted discipline is becoming increasingly evident for supervisors and supervisees alike as this alliance emphasizes the importance of continually seeking out opportunities to learn new roles, skills, and counseling approaches throughout the professional career. This practice reflects the ability to efficiently self-supervise, which is the primary goal of clinical supervision.

Providing counseling in community settings presents additional challenges as in contrast to private practice therapy. Community programs often involve therapeutic services that are rendered when a client visits the site for immediate counseling or in some cases, is court mandated. This often changes the dynamics of counseling and may even be a setting in which more resistance from a client is observed (Haynes et al., 2003). Community programs also tend to be in central locations that are in close proximity to a larger client population that reflect higher demands and therapeutic needs of diverse communities. Furthermore, certain issues such as depression, alcoholism, anxiety disorder, etc., can affect communities as a whole and community-based therapy creates a platform where helping professionals who have specialized skills can address these types of issues in the environment in which they are occurring. This prevents the progression of serious issues before they become even more problematic. Accordingly, clinical supervisors who render services through community programs are generally assigned to several supervisees, and these are only a few of the unique challenges of providing supervision in community mental health settings.

As shared communities are continuously evolving, clinical supervision must also make allowances for socio-economical changes. The Empowerment Model was established after the repeated observation that empowered supervisees are more capable of developing strong supervisory relationships and counseling skills. At the conclusion of supervision that follows this model, counselors who feel empowered also demonstrate a higher level of competence. This model is distinct from others in that it places emphasis on the different roles that supervisors naturally move through as they work with trainees. However, it also focuses on the ability of clinical counselors to identify the different levels of skills that supervisees possess at the beginning of their supervision regardless of their credentials (e.g., LPCC, LSW), and further enhance supervisees' professional attributes. These are the essential components of The Empowerment Model that equip counselors with the counseling skills that empower them to surpass expectations. The emphasis that is placed on individualized, developmental supervision is the key to effective training and it is this process that sets The Empowerment Model of Clinical Supervision apart from the more conventional clinical supervision approaches.

References

American Counseling Association (ACA). (2014). 2014 ACA Code of Ethics. Alexandria, VA: Author. Retrieved from https://www.counseling.org/Resources/aca-code-of-ethics.pdf

American Psychological Association (APA). (2015). Guidelines for clinical supervision in health service psychology. *American Psychologist, 70*, 33-46.

Association for Counselor Education and Supervision, ACES Best Practices in Clinical Supervision Taskforce. (2011). *Best practices in clinical supervision*. Retrieved from http://www.saces.org/page-1360109

Bain, S. F., Rueda, B., Mata-Villarreal, J., & Mundy, M.A. (2011). Assessing mental health needs of rural schools in South Texas: Counselors' perspectives. *Research in Higher Education Journal, 14*, 1-11.

Baker, J. G., Shanfield, S. B., & Schnee S. (2000). Using quality improvement teams to improve documentation in records at a community mental health center. *Psychiatric Services, 51*(2), 239-242.

Bardhoshi, G., & Duncan, K. (2009). Rural school principals' perceptions of the school counselor's role. *The Rural Educator, 30*(3), 16-24.

Barnett, J. E., & Molzon, C. H. (2014). Clinical supervision of psychotherapy: essential ethics issues for supervisors and supervisees. *Clinical Psychology*, *70*(11), 1051-1061.

Bean, R.A., Davis, S.D., & Davey, M.P. (2014). *Clinical supervision activities for increasing competence and self-awareness*. Hoboken, NJ: John Wiley & Sons, Inc.

Beidas, R. S., Edmunds, J. M., Cannuscio, C. C., Gallagher, M., Downey, M. M., & Kendall, P. C. (2013). Therapists perspectives on the effective elements of consultation following training. *Administration and Policy in Mental Health*, *40*(6), 507-517.

Bernard, J. M., & Goodyear, R. K. (2009). *Fundamentals of clinical supervision* (4th ed.). New York, NY: Pearson.

Bomba, J. (2011). Psychotherapy supervision as viewed from psychodynamic standpoint. *Archives of Psychiatry and Psychotherapy*, *4*, 45-49.

Borders, L. D. & Brown, L. L. (2005). *New handbook of counseling supervision*. Mahwah, NJ: Lawrence Erlbaum (1797).

Bradley, L. J., & Kottler, J. A. (2001). Overview of counselor supervision. In L. J. Bradley & N. Ladany (Eds.), *Counselor supervision: Principles, process, and practice* (pp. 3-27). New York, NY, US: Brunner-Routledge.

Bransford, J. D., & Schwartz, D. L. (2009). It takes expertise to make expertise: Some thoughts about why and how reflections on the themes in chapters 15-18. In K. A. Ericsson (Ed.), *Development of professional expertise:*

Toward measurement of expert performance and design of optimal learning environments (pp. 432-448). Cambridge, UK: Cambridge University Press.

Burg, C., Burg, J., Long, S., Melowsky, J., Pasternak, T., Rascon, C., ... Walters, C. (2017). Key factors of internship burnout and possible solutions. *Psychotherapy Bulletin*, *52*(3), 16-20.

Campbell, J. M. (2006). Essentials of clinical supervision. Hoboken, NJ: Wiley.

Colby, C., & Long, L. L. (1994). The use of a mock trial as an instructional method in counselor preparation. *Counselor Education and Supervision*, *34*(1), 58-67.

Corey G. (2012). Student manual for Corey's theory and practice of counseling and psychotherapy. Boston, MA: Cengage Learning.

Council for Accreditation of Counseling and Related Educational Programs. (2001). *CACREP accreditation standards and procedure manual*. Alexandria, VA: Author.

Davies, P. (2000). Approaches to evidence-based teaching. *Medical Teacher*, *22*(1), 14-21.

Duncan, K., Brown-Rice, K., & Bardhoshi, G. (2014). Perceptions of the importance and utilization of clinical supervision among certified rural school counselors. *Professional Counselor*, *4*(5), 444-454.

Edwards, D., Burnard, P., Hannigan, B., Cooper, L., Adams, J., Juggessur, T, Fothergil, A., & Coyle, D. (2006). Clinical supervision and burnout: the influence of clinical supervision for community mental health nurses. Journal of Clinical Nursing, *15*(8), 1007-1015.

Falender, C. A., & Shafranske, E. P. (2004). *Clinical supervision: A competency-based approach.* Washington, DC: American Psychological Association.

Falender, C. A., & Shafranske, E. P. (Eds.). (2008). *Casebook for clinical supervision: A competency-based approach*. Washington, DC, US: American Psychological Association.

Falender, C. A., & Shafranske, E. P. (2012). *Getting the most out of supervision: A guide for practicum students and interns* (1st ed.). Washington, D. C: American Psychological Association.

Feldman, R.S. (2016). *Life span development: A topical approach* (3rd ed.). New York, NY: Pearson.

Fink K. (2007). Supervision, transference and countertransference. *The International Journal of Psychoanalysis*, *88*(Pt 5), 1263-1273.

Frawley-O'Dea, M. G., & Sarnat, J. E. (2001). *The supervisory relationship: A contemporary psychodynamic approach*. New York, NY: Guilford Press.

Friedlander, M. L., & Shaffer, K. S. (2014). It's (still) all about the relationship: Relational strategies in clinical supervision. *Psychotherapy Bulletin*, *49*(4), 13-17.

Granello, D. H., Beamish, P. M., & Davis, T. E. (1997). Supervisee empowerment: Does gender make a difference? *Counselor Education and Supervision, 36,* 306-317.

Gray, S.W., & Smith, M.S. (2009). The influence of diversity in clinical supervision: A framework for reflective conversations and questioning. *The Clinical Supervisor, 28*(2), 155-179.

Green, H., Barkham, M., Kellett, S., & Saxon, D. (2014). Therapist effects and IAPT Psychological Wellbeing Practitioners (PWPs): a multilevel modelling and mixed methods analysis. *Behavior Research and Therapy, 63,* 43-54.

Hagerty, B. M., Lynch-Sauer, J., Patusky, K., & Bouwsema, M. (1993). An emerging theory of human relatedness. *Image- The Journal of Nursing Scholarship, 25*(4), 291-229.

Haynes, R., Corey, G., & Moulton, P. (2003). *Clinical supervision in the helping professions: A practical guide.* Pacific Grove, CA: Brooks/Cole.

Haynes, R., Gerald, C., & Moulton, P. (2002). *Clinical supervision in the helping professions: A practical guide.* Boston, MA: Brooks Cole.

Hipple, J., & Beamish, P. M. (2007). Supervision of counselor trainees with clients in crisis. *Journal of Professional Counseling: Practice, Theory, & Research, 35*(2), 1-16.

Hornby Zeller Associates, Inc. (2014). *West Virginia home visitation program evaluation of professional development and community collaboration.* South Portland: ME, Author. http://www.hornbyzeller.com/wp-content/uploads/2013/10/WV-Evaluation-Rept-2014-FINAL.pdf

Inman, A., Hutman, H., Pendse A., Devdas, L., Luu, L., & Ellis, M. V. (2014). Current trends concerning supervisors, supervisees, and clients in clinical supervision. In C. E. Watkins & D. L. Milne (Eds.), *The Wiley international handbook of clinical supervision* (pp. 61-102). Hoboken, NJ: John Wiley & Son, Ltd.

Johns, C., Joiner, A., Stenning, A., Latchford, Y., Madden, B., Groom, J. & Freshwater, D. (2009). Guided reflection: Advancing practice. Hoboken, NJ: Wiley-Blackwell.

Karcher, M. J., Davis, C., & Powell, B. (2002). The effects of developmental mentoring on connectedness and academic achievement. *The School Community Journal, 12*(2), 35-50.

Kearney, M. H. (1998). Truthful self-nurturing: A grounded formal theory of women's addiction. *Qualitative Health Research, 8*(4), 495-512,

Kreider, H. D. (2014). Administrative and clinical supervision: The impact of dual roles on supervisee disclosure in counseling supervision. *The Clinical Supervisor, 33*(2), 256-268.

Ladany, N., Mori, Y., & Mehr, K. E. (2013). Effective and Ineffective Supervision. *The Counseling Psychologist*, *41*(1), 28-47.

Lampropoulos, G. K. (2002). A common factors view of counseling supervision process. *The Clinical Supervisor*, *21*(1), 77-95.

Lewis, J., Arnold, M. S., House, R., & Toporek, R.L. (2002). ACA Advocacy Competencies. Alexandria, VA: American Counseling Association. Retrieved from http://www.counseling.org/Resources/Competencies/Advocacy_Competencies.pdf

Mehr, K. E., Ladany, N., & Caskie, G. L. (2010). Trainee nondisclosure in supervision: What are they not telling you? *Counseling & Psychotherapy Research*, *10*(2), 103-113.

Milne, D. L., & Reiser, R. P. (2017). A manual for evidence-based CBT supervision. Hoboken, NJ: Wiley & Sons.

National Association of Social Workers (NASW), Association of Social Work Boards (ASWB). (2013). *Best practice standards in social work supervision*. Washington, DC: National Association of Social Workers.

National Institute for Occupational Safety and Health (NIOSH). (2008). *Stress...at Work*. Cincinnati, OH: U.S. Department of Health and Human Services.

Norcross, J. C. (2011). Psychotherapy Relationships that Work: Evidence-Based Responsiveness. New York, NY: Oxford University Press.

Norcross, J. C., & Guy, J. D. Jr. (2007). *Leaving it at the Office: A Guide to Psychotherapist Self-Care*. New York, NY: The Guilford Press.

Overholser, J. (2018). *The Socratic method of psychotherapy*. New York, NY: Columbia University Press.

Parlakian, R. (2001). *Look, listen, and learn: Reflective supervision and relationship-based work*. Washington, DC: ZERO TO THREE.

Polychronis, P. D., & Brown, S. G. (2016). The strict liability standard and clinical supervision. *Professional Psychology: Research and Practice, 47*(2), 139-146.

Ratts, M. J., & Hutchins, M. A. (2009). ACA advocacy competencies: Social justice advocacy at the client/student level. *Journal of Counseling and Development, 87*(3), 269-275.

Reamer, F. (2003). Boundary issues in social work: Managing dual relationships. *Social Work. 48*(1), 121-133.

Reamer, F. (2005). Documentation in social work: Evolving ethical and risk-management standards. *Social Work, 50*(4), 325-334.

Schamess, G. (2006). Transference enactments in clinical supervision. *Clinical Social Work Journal, 34*(4), 407-425.

Shera, W., & Page, J., (1995). Creating more effective human service organizations through strategies of employment. *Administration in Social Work, 19*(4), 1-5.

Smith, G. R. Jr., Fischer, E. P., Nordquist, C. R., Mosley, C. L., & Ledbetter, N. S. (1997). Implementing outcomes management systems in mental health settings. *Psychiatric Services*, *48*(3), 364-368.

Stinchfield, T. A., Hill, N. R., & Kleist. (2011). The reflective model of triadic supervision: Defining an emerging modality. *Counselor Education and Supervision*, *46*(3), 172-183.

Substance Abuse and Mental Health Services Administration (US). (2009). *Clinical supervision and professional development of the substance abuse counselor.* Rockville, MD: SAMHSA. Retrieved from https://www.ncbi.nlm.nih.gov/books/NBK64848/

Substance Abuse and Mental Health Services Administration (SAMHSA). (2000). Treatment Improvement Protocol (TIP) Series, No. 36. Center for Substance Abuse Treatment. Rockville (MD): Author.

Todd, G., & Freshwater, D. (1999). Reflective practice and guided discovery: Clinical supervision". *British Journal of Nursing*, *8*(20), 1383-1839.

Townsend, K. C., & McWhirter, B. T. (2005). Connectedness: A review of the literature with implications for counseling, assessment, and research. *Journal of Counseling and Development*, *83*(2), 191-201.

Tromski-Klingshirn. (2007). Should the clinical supervisor be the administrative supervisor? *The Clinical Supervisor*, *25*(1-2), 53-67.

Tromski-Klingshirn, D., & Davis, T. E. (2007). Supervisees' perceptions of their clinical supervision: A study of the dual role of clinical and administrative supervisor. *Counselor Education and Supervision, 46*(4), 294-304.

Walsh, B. B., Gillespie, C., Greer, J. M., & Eanes, B. E. (2003). Influence of dyadic mutuality on counselor trainee willingness to self-disclose clinical mistakes to supervisors. *The Clinical Supervisor, 21*(2), 83-98.

Weiner, I. B., & Craighead, W. E. (2009). *The Corsini Encyclopedia of Psychology.* Hoboken, NJ: Wiley.

Wong, L. C., Wong, P. T., & Ishiyama, I. (2012). What helps and what hinders in cross-cultural clinical supervision. *The Clinical Psychologists, 41*(1):66-85.

Zimmerman, B. J., & Schunk, D. S. (2003). *Educational psychology: A century of contributions.* Mahwah, NJ: Lawrence Erlbaum Associates.

Appendix A: Engaging in Supervision

Questions to Ask in Supervision to Support Clinicians

- What goals would you like to accomplish during your supervision training?
- Can we discuss the counseling issues and topics that are currently the most pertinent to you?
- What guidelines should we establish regarding how we will work together?
- How can I help make the supervisory sessions feel like a safe place for you?
- How can we work together to help you become a more competent and confident helping professional?
- Can we establish a plan for how we will address the evaluative feedback of your counseling performance?
- How could the evaluative sessions be most helpful for you?
- What are your objectives for today's supervision meeting?
- Can you tell me about your experience while counseling that client?

- What aspects of the session with the client were important to you today?
- Can you describe the type of relationship you want to establish with the client?
- What approach do you think would best help the client?
- Do you feel like you understand the client well?
- How can I encourage you to trust your own judgement more often?
- What types of experiences have you had in the past with various cultures?
- What do you feel like you need to learn in terms of multicultural issues when working with your clients?
- What do the ethical, professional, and legal standards dictate regarding this type of issue?
- Can you tell me some different approaches to addressing this situation?
- What are some strategies you can suggest to resolve this issue?
- Which options best serve the goals and needs of the client?

Supervision Evaluation

SUPERVISION EVALUATION

Supervisee Name _____ Date of Evaluation _____

Completed by _____ Title _____

CIRCLE THE NUMBER THAT IS THE MOST APPLICABLE	REQUIRES INTERVENTION	NEEDS IMPROVEMENT	MEETS EXPECTATIONS	ABOVE EXPECTATIONS	EXCEEDS EXPECTATIONS
GENERAL SUPERVISION					
1 Demonstrates a personal commitment in developing professional competencies.	1	2	3	4	5
2 Invests time and energy in becoming a proficient therapist.	1	2	3	4	5
3 Accepts and uses feedback to enhance self-development and counseling skills.	1	2	3	4	5
4 Engages in open, comfortable, and clear communication with supervisor.	1	2	3	4	5
5 Recognizes own competencies and skills and shares these with supervisor.	1	2	3	4	5
6 Completes case reports and records punctually and conscientiously.	1	2	3	4	5
7 Actively seeks feedback and consultation from supervisor.	1	2	3	4	5
8 Recognizes own deficiencies and actively works to overcome them with peers and supervisor.	1	2	3	4	5

THE ADMINISTRATIVE COUNSELING PROCESS					
9 Researches the referral prior to intake.	1	2	3	4	5
10 Keeps appointments on time, minimal cancels/reschedules.	1	2	3	4	5
11 Schedules intake promptly.	1	2	3	4	5
12 Explains the nature and objective of services when necessary.	1	2	3	4	5
13 Communicates interest in and acceptance of clients.	1	2	3	4	5
14 Refers to clients in a strength-based manner.	1	2	3	4	5

THE CLINICAL COUNSELING PROCESS					
15 Facilitates clients' expressions of concerns and feelings.	1	2	3	4	5
16 Focuses on the contents of the client's problems.	1	2	3	4	5
17 Recognizes clients' manipulation and handles it appropriately.	1	2	3	4	5
18 Is aware of own feelings during sessions.	1	2	3	4	5
19 Communicates own feelings to client when appropriate (immediacy).	1	2	3	4	5
20 Uses self-disclosure appropriately.	1	2	3	4	5
21 Facilitates realistic goals with clients.	1	2	3	4	5
22 Completes realistic treatment plans, within a timely manner.	1	2	3	4	5
23 Indicates periodic evaluation of goals and processes during services.	1	2	3	4	5
24 Terminates clients appropriately.	1	2	3	4	5

Croswaite Brindle & Murphy

CIRCLE THE NUMBER THAT IS THE MOST APPLICABLE	REQUIRES INTERVENTION	NEEDS IMPROVEMENT	MEETS EXPECTATIONS	ABOVE EXPECTATIONS	EXCEEDS EXPECTATIONS
THE CONCEPTUALIZATION PROCESS					
25 Focuses on specific behaviors and their consequences.	1	2	3	4	5
26 Recognizes and pursues descriptions and meaning of inconsistent information.	1	2	3	4	5
27 Uses relevant case data in planning both immediate and long range goals.	1	2	3	4	5
28 Uses relevant case data in considering various strategies and their implications.	1	2	3	4	5
29 Discusses case data with supervisor when developing goals.	1	2	3	4	5
30 Recognizes personal bias and addresses as needed.	1	2	3	4	5
31 Demonstrates understanding of ethical standards with cases.	1	2	3	4	5

PROFESSIONAL COMMUNICATION					
32 Communicates with professional team to move a case forward.	1	2	3	4	5
33 Emails monthly reports/updates on time to professional team.	1	2	3	4	5
34 Notifies professional team of referral assignment in a timely manner.	1	2	3	4	5
35 Emails professional team as needed to communicate concerns.	1	2	3	4	5
36 Formulates goals to professional team goals for client/family.	1	2	3	4	5
37 Checks in with supervisor on a consistent basis.	1	2	3	4	5
38 Checks professional email several times a day.	1	2	3	4	5
39 Addresses concerns immediately.	1	2	3	4	5

Additional Feedback _____

_____

_____

_____

_____

_____

Supervisor Signature _____ Date _____

By signing this form, I am indicating that I have read this report and have discussed its content with my supervisor.

Supervisee Signature _____ Date _____

Adapted from Griffith Centers for Children

To download a printable version, please visit our website at

empowermentmodelsupervision.com

Professional Disclosure Statement for Supervision

Thank you for selecting me as your clinical supervisor. The purpose of this form is to ensure a common understanding about the supervision process.

Professional Disclosure

I earned a PhD in Counseling Psychology from North Carolina University and am a licensed mental health counselor, licensed marriage and family therapist and an approved supervisor in the state of Michigan. I am a member of the Association for Humanistic Psychology and the Michigan Mental Health Counselors Association. I have worked in an agency and private practice since 1983 and I teach in North Carolina University's Masters in Psychology program. My theoretical orientation for counseling and supervision combines humanistic, transpersonal, psychodynamic and developmental theories.

Explanation of Dual Relationships

To adequately work on your professional development, we need to meet on a regular basis. We would usually meet weekly for a fifty-minute hour unless we have made other arrangements. Fees will be determined prior to the initial session. Fees may vary based on my perception of current going rates and any agreement that I may come to with you. If you miss a scheduled session with less than 24 hours notice, you will be charged for that session.

If you need to speak to me between sessions or in case of a client emergency, you may call me at my office. I will get back to you as soon as possible. I check voicemail frequently during the weekdays and several times over the weekends. If I am out of town we will arrange for you to have the contact information of a licensed clinician who will be available to you in my absence.

Supervision Process

My goal is for your supervision to be a rewarding and caring experience. It is an interactive process that improves the quality of client care, increases your clinical skills and nurtures your professional growth. You can expect to receive timely feedback about your interventions and to have a supportive environment in which to explore client-related concerns, inclusive of transference issues that invariably arise.

As I am legally responsible as are you, for the quality of clinical care you provide, you may be asked to do readings, attend certain classes, or participate in additional supervision hours if education is needed for you to adequately practice as a therapist. You may be asked to bring in audio or videotapes of your work. These potential growth areas are designed to improve your counseling competencies and support your professional identity. I invite you to ask questions, explore alternatives, address ethical concerns and receive feedback and suggestions on your counseling interventions.

Legally, you must notify your clients that you are receiving supervision from me. Your clients will need to sign an agreement permitting you to receive supervision either as part of your client disclosure form or in a separate document. Thus, all parties are informed about our supervision relationship.

Supervision is not intended to provide you with personal counseling or therapy. If personal issues or concerns arise that seem to negatively affect your clinical practice, I may ask you to seek personal psychotherapy.

Confidentiality

The content of our sessions and evaluations are confidential with certain exceptions. Limits to confidentiality include but are not limited to, treatment of a client that violates the legal or ethical standards set forth by professional associations and government agencies, and disclosures agreed upon in the Agency Supervision Agreement if we have signed one. I also have the ethical responsibility to require you to have additional supervision if necessary to bring your practice up to minimal standards. While I don't anticipate needing to do any of these things, it is in the interest of good supervision to be clear about our respective responsibilities.

Fee per session_____ Date _____.

I, _____, have read and understand the above policy & disclosure statement.

_____

Print supervisee name

_____   _____

Supervisee signature   *Date*

_____   _____

Supervisor signature   *Date*

Name _____

Work #_____Cell #_____
Home #_____

Address_____ City_____
ZIP_____

Emergency Name _____
Phone: _____

To download a printable version, please visit our website at empowermentmodelsupervision.com

Individual Development Plan for Clinical Supervision

Supervisee: _____

Supervisor: _____

Date developed: _____Date of review:
_____

Learning Goal/Need	Plan	Criteria	Supervision Method	Outcome

Supervisee Signature: _____

Date _____

Supervisor Signature: _____

Date _____

To download a printable version, please visit our website at

empowermentmodelsupervision.com

Appendix B: Resources for Supervision
Agency Letterhead
(To be completed by Supervisee)

Weekly/Bi-Weekly Clinical Supervision

Supervisee:
Supervisor:

Topics discussed:			
Duties & expectations	Comprehensive skills evaluation	Cases & Assessment	Information & referral
Professionalism	Process recording	High Risk issues	Evaluation issues
Judgment	Decision making	Progress notes	Termination
Communication skills	Problem solving	Goals & objectives	Diversity issues
Counseling topics & deadlines	Initiative	Practice/Intervention skills	Mezzo practice issues
Attitude	Flexibility	Crisis intervention	Macro practice issues
Time management	Self-awareness	Treatment planning	Ethical issues
Learning plan	Accountability	Specific ACA techniques	Other:

Comments:

_____

_____

_____

Supervisee Strengths:

_____

_____

_____

Challenges:

_____

_____

_____

Tasks to be completed by the next supervision session or date specified:

_____

_____

_____

Supervisee Signature: _____

Date _____

Supervisee Signature: _____

Date _____

To download a printable version, please visit our website at

empowermentmodelsupervision.com

Critical Incident Report
Agency Letterhead

(To be completed by Supervisee)

Your Name: _____

Agency site: _____

Date and time the incident occurred:

_____

Names of clients and/or individuals involved:

_____

_____

Witness(es) to incident, if applicable:

_____

_____

Location of incident (e.g., individual, family session):

_____

Brief description of incident: As accurately as possible, record what each person did and said. Include your own role in the event.

Describe the actions you took to report this event to the Agency Supervisor:

210

Sign and submit this form to your Supervisor.

Supervisee Signature: _____ Date _____

Supervisor Signature: _____

Date _____

To download a printable version, please visit our website at

empowermentmodelsupervision.com

Court Testimony Preparation Questionnaire*

1. Name
2. Occupation
3. Where are you currently employed? For how long?
4. Please summarize your educational background
5. Please summarize your professional experience
6. How are you acquainted with the client? Your role with the client?
7. How is the therapeutic service you offer defined (e.g. family therapy, individual)?
8. What kind of caseload do you have while providing counseling in your current role?
9. What goals do you have in counseling with this client? What progress has been made towards those goals?
10. What were strengths in your work with this client?
11. What were challenges in your work with this client?
12. What documentation or records are kept to reflect progress?

13. What period of time have you provided counseling with this client? Approximately how many sessions?

14. What observations do you have of the client? Diagnoses?

15. What recommendations do you have for this client moving forward?

*These questions do not represent an exhaustive list and are not legal advice. Please consult your attorney or malpractice insurance entity for further preparation and legal consultation.

To download a printable version, please visit our website at

empowermentmodelsupervision.com

Appendix C: Risk Management Tools for Counseling

Suicide Risk Assessment
Agency Letterhead

Have you thought about suicide?   Yes or No

Do you have a plan? Yes or No

Do you have access to means? (firearms, pills, etc.)

Yes or No

How often are the thoughts? How difficult to control?

Intensity?

_____

_____

What would that look like to you? _____-

_____

What would that mean to you?

_____

Preparatory Acts? Yes or No   If yes, please describe

_____

_____

Rehearsal? Yes or No

Aborted Attempts? Yes or No

Interrupted Attempts? Yes or No

Do you engage in Non-Suicidal Self-Injury (NSSI)?

Yes or No

If yes, what does NSSI do for you?

_____

Do you know someone who has completed suicide? Yes or

No

If yes, who _____

Do you have a family history of suicide? Yes or No

What current behaviors? (poor hygiene, isolation, avoidance, preparatory acts)

_____

_____

_____

_____

What current symptoms? (burden, isolation, hopelessness, anxiety, depression, impulsivity, etc.)

_____

_____

_____

_____

Initial Level of Risk: Low   Moderate   High

Professional Consultation/Supervision/Staffing:

_____

_____

_____

_____

Determined Level of Risk: Low   Moderate   High

Next Steps:

Engaged Supports:
_____

Action Steps Taken:

_____

_____

_____

_____

Safety Planning Completed: Yes or No
Resources Given:
_____

Documentation Completed
_____

Supervisee Signature: _____
Date _____
Supervisee Signature: _____
Date _____

To download a printable version, please visit our website at

empowermentmodelsupervision.com

Individual Safety Plan
Agency Letterhead

Step 1: Warning signs: (thoughts, mood, behavior changes, negative images)

1. _____

2. _____

3. _____

Step 2: Internal coping strategies - Things I can do to take my mind off my problems without contacting another person: (go for a walk, go to the gym, go see a funny movie)

1. _____

2. _____

3. _____

Step 3: People and social settings that provide distraction:

1. Name _____
   Phone _____

2. Name _____
   Phone _____

3. Place _____

4. Place _____

Step 4: People whom I can ask for help:

1. Name _____
   Phone _____

2. Name _____
   Phone _____

3. Name _____
   Phone _____

Step 5: Professionals or agencies I can contact during a crisis:

1. Clinician Name _____
   Phone   _____
   Emergency   _____

2. Clinician Name _____
   Phone   _____
   Emergency   _____

3. Local Urgent Care Services

_____

Urgent Care Services Address

_____

Urgent Care Services Phone

_____

4. Suicide Prevention Resource Name

_____

Suicide Prevention Resource Phone   _____

5.Suicide Prevention Hotline Phone: 1-800-273-TALK

Step 6: Making the environment safe:

1. _____

2. _____

Supervisee Signature: _____
Date _____
Supervisee Signature: _____
Date _____

To download a printable version, please visit our website at

empowermentmodelsupervision.com

Family Safety Plan
Agency Letterhead

Contact and Resources

Support Person _____
Phone   _____

Babysitter   _____
Phone   _____

Team daytime _____
Phone   _____

Team On-Call _____
Phone   _____

Notes:

Plan Goal

Example: We all agree to pay close attention to when our physical behavior is getting worse in order to try new coping strategies and use them while in public.

Actions

If this happens, try this technique:

If she slams door and yells...   Give her a clear and short warning

If the warning does not work... Tell her to wait in her room while call a support person or team member

Strategies for Making the Environment Safe

<u>Identify an in-home support team</u>

<u>Avoid a   power struggle</u>

Supervisee Signature: _____

Date _____

Supervisee Signature: _____

Date _____

To download a printable version, please visit our website at

empowermentmodelsupervision.com

Index

C
CACREP
pp. 7, 12

Center for Credentialing and Education
pp. 12

Client welfare
pp. 7, 18, 20, 29, 31-33, 38, 97, 99, 140, 174

Clinician self
pp. 54, 85-89

Clinical supervision, definition
pp. 8-11

Collaboration
pp. 17, 79-82, 148-150

Colleague referrals
pp. 113

Community contact
pp. 112, 190

Conflict between supervisor and supervisee
pp. 22, 33, 119, 120, 124

Confidentiality
pp. 15, 95, 112, 113, 138-143, 154, 157, 158, 166, 168-171, 213 86, 107-116, 121-126, 134-138, 168, 172-175, 183, 192

Community
pp. 13, 112, 146-150, 155-157, 173, 179, 193-194

Post-Graduates
pp. 31, 40

Psychodynamic supervision
pp. 13, 20-23

R
Reality perspective
pp. 77-79

Redirection
pp. 110, 124, 125

Reflection
pp. 14-16, 66-72, 75, 115, 191

Reflective supervision
pp. 13, 14, 16, 20

Release of information
pp. 113, 143, 168

Researcher
pp. 45, 52, 53, 59, 92, 98, 104, 106, 186, 189

S
Secondary referrals
pp. 112

Self-care
pp. 59, 82-89, 136-138

Self-supervise
pp. 11, 32, 81, 192

Glossary

<u>Child Protective Services (CPS)</u>: Also known at Child Welfare Services, a governmental division tasked with investigating cases of alleged abuse and neglect involving children.

<u>Department of Human Services (DHS)</u>: A department that is run by state and county funding to provide adults and families access to community resources including but not limited to housing support, childcare, disability services, and benefits assistance.

<u>Dependency and Neglect (D&N)/Abuse and Neglect Case</u>: Describes open cases involving child abuse and neglect.

<u>Guardian Ad Litem (GAL)</u>: A legal representative appointed by the courts to identify represent a child's best interests in response to legal needs, parental disputes, or cases of abuse and neglect.

<u>Mandated Reporter</u>: A person identified by his or her profession, who is required by law to report any suspicion or allegation of child abuse and neglect to authorities in order to reduce possible cases of child abuse and neglect.

Made in the USA
Middletown, DE
30 July 2019